YOU CAN CHANGE THE FUTURE

YOU CAN CHANGE THE FUTURE

BRIAN HOUSTON

PUBLISHED BY MAXIMISED LEADERSHIP INC.

YOU CAN CHANGE THE FUTURE
First published July 2000

Copyright © 2000 Brian Houston

All rights reserved. No part of this publication may be reproduced in any form or by any means without prior written permission from the publisher.

National Library of Australia:
Cataloguing-in-Publication data:

> Houston, Brian.
> You can change the future : living beyond today and impacting the generations ahead.
>
> ISBN 0 9577336 2 3.
>
> 1. Life skills. 2. Change. 3. Conduct of life. 4. Self-help techniques. I. Title.
>
> 158.1

Scripture taken from the New King James Version. Copyright © 1982 by Thomas Nelson, Inc. Used by permission. All rights reserved.

Bold emphasis in scriptures is author's own.

Cover design by CPGD,
Suite 19, 226-271 Pennant Hills Road,
Thornleigh, NSW 2120 Australia

Back cover photographs by Femia Shirtliffe.
Photo of Ben, Brian and Joel Houston

Printed by J S McMillan Printing, Lidcombe, NSW, Australia

Published by Maximised Leadership Incorporated,
PO Box 1195, Castle Hill, NSW 1765 Australia

**LIVING BEYOND TODAY
AND IMPACTING THE
GENERATIONS AHEAD**

Three generations of the Houston family – Brian Houston with his father Frank, and eldest son, Joel. (Photo taken in 1998)

DEDICATION

To my parents, Frank and Hazel Houston,
whose decisions in life
changed not only their own future,
but *my* future, as well as
the lives of countless thousands of
men and women across the globe.

CONTENTS

INTRODUCTION		1
PART 1: THE POWER TO CHANGE		5
Chapter 1:	Change the story of your life	9
Chapter 2:	Change the theme of your heart	13
Chapter 3:	Change your test into a testimony	17
Chapter 4:	Change a mess into a message	23
Chapter 5:	Change the course of your life	27
Chapter 6:	Change your expectations	31
PART 2: CHANGE THE POWER OF EXCUSES		37
Chapter 7:	Change your ways	41
Chapter 8:	Change your decision-making process	45
Chapter 9:	Change your focus	49
Chapter 10:	Change your excuses	53
Chapter 11:	Change your excuse nature	59
PART 3: CHANGE THE POWER OF THE PAST		63
Chapter 12:	Change the power of secrecy	67
Chapter 13:	Change through repentance	73
Chapter 14:	Change a curse into a blessing	77
Chapter 15:	Change the parenting process	81
PART 4: CHANGE THE POWER OF TODAY		87
Chapter 16:	Change your future – day by day	91
Chapter 17:	Change your attitude towards today	95
Chapter 18:	Change the quality of each day	99
Chapter 19:	Change the value of your days	105

PART 5: THE POWER TO CHANGE THE FUTURE   109
Chapter 20: Change the impact of yesterday on today   113
Chapter 21: Change to live days with hope   117
Chapter 22: Change the impact on the generations   121
Chapter 23: Change that influences others   125
Chapter 24: Change your commitments   129
Chapter 25: Change your priorities   135

CONCLUSION   139
FOOTNOTE REFERENCES   147

INTRODUCTION

INTRODUCTION

When my father was 18 years old, he was a disillusioned teenager with no sense of purpose. He was almost an alcoholic, sick in his body and depressed about life, yet something happened that changed his life forever.

It was at the funeral of a close school friend that he heard the Gospel and was challenged to make a choice there and then. He gave his life to Jesus Christ and discovered a new, exciting way of living.

That decision made back in 1940 was the major turning point that set him on a path and destiny that has had far-reaching effect. It not only changed his life, but it set a new course for the future generations of the Houston family. Yet it doesn't stop there. Frank Houston has served God for over fifty years and the impact of his preaching and ministry has ultimately changed the lives of countless thousands around the world.

Growing up in the church as I did, I have seen God at work in people's lives. Not only do I know that He can change lives, but I know that He wants to and does. Making the decision to invite God into your life sets the course for a great future and a great destiny.

Life is full of options, choices and opportunities. We were not created to be robots or puppets, but rather free-thinking, creative individuals who have the capacity to fulfil great potential. I believe God has a plan and purpose for each and every life that will ultimately lead to the complete fulfilment of one's destiny.

There are three types of people: those who *watch* things happen, those who *make* things happen, and those who *wonder* what happened. Frank Houston went from watching and wondering about life, to making things happen. It began with making a significant decision which changed him forever.

We were created to live life to its maximum capacity. We were not created to be observers or bystanders, but rather active participants over the entire spectrum of the days allotted to us.

Being a Bible-believing Christian is all about discovering principles that enable you to live an exciting life of purpose, full of vision and hope. The Old Testament prophet Jeremiah, prophesied the words of God:

> 'For I know the thoughts that I think toward you, says the Lord, thoughts of peace and not of evil, to give you **a future and a hope.**'[1]

No matter what circumstances you may be facing now, God has a great future in mind for you. You don't have to watch your life unfold in helpless bewilderment. You can change the future! It's a powerful statement but it's true. You may not like your past, or you may be disillusioned with your present situation, but the exciting fact is that you can look forward with hope and expectancy to your future, because you *can* do something about it. The exciting impact of changing your future goes well beyond you, because when *you* change your life, the lives of many others are also changed.

The ultimate question before you begin reading this book is, **do you want more from your life?** If you are fed up with your job, unhappy with your personality, disillusioned with your relationships or bored with your lifestyle – you *can* change it! It only takes a spark to get a fire going. Hopefully the following chapters will ignite you to change, and in doing so, will launch you into an exciting new future.

YOU CAN CHANGE THE FUTURE

PART ONE

THE POWER TO CHANGE

**Everyone thinks of changing
the world, but no-one thinks of
changing himself**

(Leo Tolstoy)

CHAPTER ONE

CHANGE THE STORY OF YOUR LIFE

I was born in a Salvation Army hospital for unwed mothers in New Zealand. For the record, my parents were married, but as Salvation Army officers, that's where their children were born. During the course of my childhood, we moved house frequently and I ended up going to seven different schools. Being the middle child of five children was especially interesting. I guess that's *the story of my life* ...

No, it's not actually. Even though the facts are true, the reality is that the story of my life has been one of adventure and excitement. I've loved my life so far, and it just keeps getting better.

"That's the story of my life"

A few years ago, I was at the Sydney airport with my wife Bobbie and good friend Pat Mesiti, when the following incident took place. While standing in line to pick up my ticket, a man behind me was becoming frantic because he reckoned that his plane was almost about to depart. Generously I allowed him to go before me, and never thought any more of it until we reached the final departure lounge. I went to get myself a cup of coffee, and there before me was the panic-stricken passenger ... also getting himself a cup of coffee.

I couldn't resist saying to him, "I thought your plane was about to leave."

You'd have thought that I'd bitten him, because he turned around in fury, and said "Well, my plane *is* about to leave," shoving his ticket and his boarding pass in my face. As he carried on getting his coffee, the PA system suddenly broadcast the following announcement: "This is an urgent call for Professor So-and-so. Please proceed immediately to departure gate three because your plane is ready to depart."

He turned to me in triumphant satisfaction. "See, I told you – my plane *is* about to depart."

"Well, you'd better go and catch it then," I said, and began to wander off. But he came after me.

"This is the story of my life!" he said "I'm probably going to miss my plane because of you. You were probably the high school bully. It's people like you who have caused the problem in Bosnia." According to this man, the war in Bosnia was *my* fault!

As the PA system called out his name again, I turned and said, "You'd better go and catch your plane." He continued ranting and raving at Bobbie, Pat and me, as we all said in unison "Go and catch your plane!" Finally he gathered his belongings and headed for the door, muttering as he went, while we sat back and enjoyed our coffee.

Next minute the door was flung open, and there he stood, completely enraged. "See, I told you. I've missed my plane!"

Whenever I recall that incident, I marvel how an intelligent professor could become so ruled by such a minor, negative detail in life. The truth is, many people are, and consequently miss many awesome opportunities in life.

"That's the story of my life!" How often have you heard someone make a statement like that? One may claim with a sigh of resignation, "I'm always unlucky in love, but that's the story of my life" or another will say, "I always seem to have cashflow problems; it is just my lot in life!" Generally people seem to base the story of their life around negative circumstances.

You may have experienced a setback in life such as a failed marriage or a financial disaster, but that doesn't necessarily constitute the 'story of your life.' That event may carry its consequences, but it's only a single episode and it doesn't have to set the tone of your entire life.

There are those however, who marry and divorce several times, and what you witness emerging is a cycle or a pattern that could easily become the story of their life. Others may have experienced a succession of business failures, and the chain reaction of recurring problems seems to become their lot in life.

However, the good news is that you *can* break the cycle and change the pattern because God has an awesome plan and destiny in store for you. You can begin to change the future by changing the story of your life.

Every story has a theme

Every story is written according to a *theme*, and that theme is what recurs repeatedly. For instance, this book is all about changing the future, so you'll find that every chapter is linked to this theme. In the same way, the story of your life is based on the recurring theme that runs through your life.

The recurring story of someone's life is connected to the *theme of one's heart*. The psalmist wrote:

My **heart** is overflowing with a good theme. [2]

What happens in your life is an overflow of what is inside your heart. If your heart overflows with negativity and defeat, then that is what will spill out and consequently affect your life. I'm not talking about one-off tragedies or mistakes that can happen to any of us, but rather that recurring pattern or theme. In the same way, if your heart overflows with generosity and love, that is what will colour your world.

I have great respect for people who have overcome tremendous obstacles and still rise to success. There are countless testimonies of ordinary people who made their mark on the world by doing extraordinary feats in the face of adversity. What separates them from average people who succumb to external pressures? The key lies in what is inside them.

Human nature has a tendency to only deal with the *external issues* of life, and many people respond accordingly. Often their solution to an unhappy relationship or marriage is to walk away, or their solution to financial or business pressure is to uproot and move to another place. One who is feeling disillusioned and depressed may resort to a new haircut or wardrobe to boost their spirits, but all these responses are in fact avoiding the real issue.

> What lies behind us and what lies before us are tiny matters compared to what lies within us.
> – Ralph Waldo Emerson

Internal factors and the deeper issues are what dictate our life, and this is where many people encounter difficulty. They'll be quick to change the *outward*, but what is really needed is a change from *within*. The internal, not the external, needs to change ... and that is what so many avoid.

You may be going through tough times, and your life may seem to be a mess, but you can turn a test into a testimony, a mess into a message and a trial into triumph. God has an incredible plan and story for your life. Don't settle for mediocrity when mega-opportunity is yours to experience. Determine to change your future today.

CHANGE
THE STORY OF YOUR LIFE

CHAPTER TWO

CHANGE THE THEME OF YOUR HEART

I have flown across the Pacific Ocean between Sydney and Los Angeles countless times. It is a 14 hour, non-stop flight and because it crosses the International Date Line, you actually end up getting there two or three hours before you left!

Because flying is such a regular occurrence in my life, I am very familiar with the whole procedure. I trust the pilots and the technology they use to get us to our destination at the expected time.

But if the pilot made the following announcement, I admit I'd be a little worried: "Ladies and gentlemen, I don't want you to be too concerned, but our radar system is down. Nevertheless, we are looking out the window into the darkness. We know that Los Angeles is in the general direction we are heading, so we are confident that we will eventually get you to your destination."

Since planes are designed to fly according to the *way their system is set*, I'd have reason to be concerned. Without the instruments working, it would definitely be a hit-and-miss affair. We would certainly end up flying off course.

In the very same way, your life will follow the course your

heart has set for you. Your heart has the capacity to plan your way.

> A man's heart plans his way, but the Lord directs his steps.[3]

This proverb almost sounds like a contradiction, but if your heart chooses to line up with the steps the Lord has planned for your life, you will see the purposes of God fulfilled. If you choose to be filled with the fullness of God, your heart will set new boundaries, borders and parameters. They will then set you on course to live the exceedingly, abundant life the Bible talks about.

Instruction from the heart

God has pre-planned and pre-designed an incredible life for you, but your heart has *to choose* that course. So many people end up living short of God's best for them, because the power working in them prevents them from finding the path that will cause their full potential to be realised. There will be times in your life when you will be faced with decisions and won't know which way to turn. You could end up disorientated or confused, feeling lost and fearful. It is then that your heart will need to instruct and guide you correctly.

> I will bless the Lord who has given me counsel; My heart also instructs me in the **night seasons**.[4]

From time to time, every one of us will be confronted with a 'night season.' It is difficult to see in the dark, and during those confusing times, your heart will instruct you according to what it knows. I once heard someone say that it is in adversity that a man is introduced to himself. If your heart only knows panic, insecurity or rejection, then that is the instruction it will give you.

Don't neglect your inner man. Your reaction to adversity and opposition is a great revealer of where your heart is set. Some people emerge through difficult times and keep moving forward, while others spiral downwards. What is in their heart is directing their outcome. How many times have you witnessed people encounter financial prosperity, only to watch their heart shrink it down to nothing because they couldn't deal with the challenges?

We all need to address the theme of our hearts because it has the power to write the story of our lives. There is a proverb that gives us wise instruction about the condition of our heart:

> Keep your heart with all diligence, for out of it spring the **issues** of life. [5]

The issues of our life are not totally defined by our education, whether we know the right people, or whether we are in the right place at the right time. The borders or parameters of our life are not related to external things, but rather internal things. The recurring story of our life unfolds according to the theme of our heart. The Word warns us to guard our hearts, because it relates to how we live our lives.

Jesus said that it is not what goes into a person that defiles them, it is that which comes out.

> A good man out of the good treasure of his heart brings forth good things, and an evil man out of the evil treasure brings forth evil things. [6]

Out of a heart of faith comes faith, and out of an overcoming spirit comes the ability to overcome. Yet someone who has a defeated, negative heart will bring forth a spirit of negativity and defeat, and will sadly live with the consequences of that recurring theme.

What's inside will come out

What are you full of? When you are squeezed, what comes out? Paul wrote to the Ephesians, encouraging them to be filled with all the fullness of God (Ephesians 3:19). He continued to explain that being full of God enables Him to do exceedingly abundantly above all that we ask or think, according to *the power* that works in us (Ephesians 3:20).

What you fill your life with, determines the power at work in you. If you are filled with hurt, anger, bitterness or negativity, then that becomes the power that influences your life. Those however, who are filled with the power of God are enabling Him to do exceedingly more than we could ask or think of.

Unexpected challenges or adversity should not *rule* your life. If you establish the right principles within, you can without doubt change these situations.

Have you ever watched people who develop a victim mentality to life, because they have allowed themselves to become defeated and down-trodden? Ruled by external factors, they are quick to blame the economy, their parents, the stock market or the church for their circumstances. By allowing that disillusionment and discouragement to rule them, that now becomes the power that works in their lives.

No matter what circumstances you may be facing, deal with the issues of the heart and begin to overflow with that good theme. Your heart has the powerful capacity to instruct you, so be sure it instructs you in a positive and life-changing way.

Changing the theme of your heart doesn't mean you won't have adversity or challenges, but like a plane in the midst of a storm, it will stay on the course set, and will see you through to the other side.

CHANGE
THE THEME OF YOUR HEART

CHAPTER THREE

CHANGE YOUR TEST INTO A TESTIMONY

Over the years I watched a certain couple in our church struggle under the pressures that their business was facing. Due to unforeseen circumstances, they found themselves with a debt that amounted to a six figure sum.

They had two options: either to throw in the towel and file for bankruptcy, or to stick it out and find ways to pay off the debt. Being Bible-believing, faith-filled Christians, they had set their course in life, and chose to take up the challenge. Month after month, they diligently worked towards paying off the debt, always faithful and putting God first in their lives.

It wasn't easy, and there were times when the weight of the debt felt as if it was crushing them. But they persevered with determination to see it through. Then, just when they wondered whether they were going to make it, a miracle happened. They received a contract that injected a massive sum of money into their business. Overnight, their situation turned around.

I love hearing stories like that, when tests are turned into testimonies. Instead of surrendering to defeat and failure, it takes determination to change the course of one's life and the outcome of the future.

Decide you have had enough

Deciding that you have had enough is the first step towards changing your mess into a message and your test into a testimony. It's all about reaching a point of desperation where you say, "Enough is enough!" This is the turning point.

> When it becomes more difficult to suffer than to change ... you will change. – Dr Robert Anthony

How far would you go down the road of disaster before you decided to do anything about it? Things began to change in the life of the prodigal son when he reached rock bottom. He had squandered his inheritance and ended up living with the pigs, but then the Bible says that he "came to himself" (Luke 15:17). He came to his senses and decided it would be a better option to return home to his father's house. In other words, he had had *had enough*.

It never ceases to amaze me how those in the midst of a crisis will say how much they want their circumstances to change, but they don't make any effort to facilitate that change. You watch them making the same mistakes, the same bad decisions and going down the same old road over and over again.

> Some people change their ways when they see the light, others when they feel the heat.
> – Caroline Schoeder

Grow up

One of the reasons why some people live in a continual state of chaos is simply because of *immaturity*. Children are capable of irresponsible decisions but it's amazing how many adults can be grown-up on the outside, yet so immature on the inside.

Sadly, some marriages do break down, but there are times when this could have been avoided. At the altar, a couple vows, "for better, for worse, for richer, for poorer." There are those who, when facing a tough situation in their marriage, are inclined to opt out. It is rather like a child who declares when the game isn't going their way, "Well, I'm not going to play anymore."

The same applies to finances. If you keep on spending money that you don't have, you will end up in deep financial trouble. The real issue is immaturity and irresponsibility. All it requires is a little common sense: if you don't have it, don't spend it.

> Life is change. Growth is optional. Choose wisely.
> – Karen Kaiser Clark

The Word of God teaches us how to live wisely. By growing up in the ways of God, you can change the process of your life.

Change how you see yourself

One of the greatest keys to changing your circumstances, is changing the way you *see yourself*. It's a fact – people live their lives according to how they see themselves. If you have a low self-esteem and poor sense of self-worth, you'll have an inferiority complex that will keep you contained.

Take the example of a beautiful young girl who has a good education and great future ahead of her. However, she involves herself with a loser, and everyone wonders why. The reality is that she is making choices according to the way she sees herself – a poor self-esteem *positioning* her with someone way below her potential.

You will always place limitations on your life if you have a limited self-perception. I once told someone about the opportunity I had to speak at the opening of the Australian Parliament in 1998. They asked me if I had been nervous, because they couldn't see themselves doing that. Now there was a time when I also couldn't have pictured myself doing that because of the way I viewed myself.

You need to get a bigger or more expansive picture of God. If all you see is what God *did* in Bible days, or what He *will* do in heaven, you will never be able to see that He has the answers for you *today*.

Have a vision

Having a vision or a dream for your life is perhaps the greatest *destiny protector* I know. Vision is about having a sense of purpose and knowing that your life is going somewhere. Never let anything destroy or rob your dream. Cynicism may try, and others may try and pull you down to size.

Without purpose, people live carelessly and irresponsibly. Having a vision is a powerful weapon or tool in anyone's hand. It is something that can help you change, so pursue it and protect it from being stolen.

Accept wise counsel

Over the years, I've seen people dive into situations, regardless of good and godly counsel. There have been couples who, within days of meeting, are convinced that they should get married. Counsel from people who care may caution them to slow down, yet they choose not to listen.

People are always on the lookout for short cuts and after they've taken them, wonder why they ended up in a mess. There will be times when you may have to change your decisions according to the wisdom of godly counsel. It is far more important that your life lines up with the Word of God.

We will take a closer look at those who speak into and influence your life in a later chapter.

Lighten up

My wife, Bobbie, and I once sat chatting to a couple who had made some major mistakes in their life and just couldn't seem to get out of the mess. As a result, they were so intense and uptight, and both had concluded that life wasn't meant to be easy.

Their whole theology and faith had been brought down to the level of their somewhat miserable experience. Sensing their spirit of hopelessness and defeat, Bobbie's spontaneous counsel to them was simple: "You guys need to go out and have some fun!"

Sometimes that is what you need to do in the midst of a test or trial in your life. Lighten up and position yourself around some free-spirited people who are enjoying life.

If you are going to turn your test into a testimony, make sure your heart lines up with the steps that God has directed for your life. As your heart begins to plan a different course for your life, you will *emerge* from the test and discover a new story for your life beginning to unfold.

CHANGE YOUR TEST INTO A TESTIMONY

CHAPTER FOUR

CHANGE
A MESS INTO A MESSAGE

Every week, during our weekend church services, we read out prayer requests and praise reports. Prayer requests are written on yellow slips of paper while praise reports are green. It is our desire that every yellow prayer request will eventually become a green praise report.

The needs of our congregation vary, from asking us to pray for employment, finances or an uncertain future to those in desperate need of a miracle. As a pastor, it saddens me to see those who are under attack, battling life-threatening diseases, family breakups and other tragedies.

Yet there is nothing I like better than reading from the praise reports, bearing testimony to the fact that God has turned a seemingly hopeless situation around. The tumour disappeared … husband and wife were reconciled … surgery wasn't necessary … a new job with double the salary …!

The best thing about praise reports is how they stir up faith, and are evidence that God is alive and well, working in people's lives today.

At some point you may go through a test or trial in your life – it could be your finances, a relationship or your emotional stability. Asking others to pray for you is always a step in the right direction, because God is longing to see you living a blessed, victorious life in Him. He is in the life-changing business. In Christ, a mess can become a powerful message.

How do people get into a mess?

I've often wondered how people get themselves into such situations. It is actually quite simple, and I am going to show you how. If I can show you how people get *into* such situations, it may help you avoid or understand how to get *out* (and stay out) of them.

The underlying problem is that many people refuse to *confront issues* and see them for what they are. Because of this, they often go from one mess to the next, and never break the cycle.

Don't allow the enemy room to move

One of the main reasons why people end up in a mess is because they give the enemy room to move.

While God has a great future in mind for you, the enemy is doing everything he can to prevent you from achieving it. The scripture is very clear about the devil's job description. Jesus said that he comes to "steal, kill and destroy" (John 10:10). His objective is to get you into a mess and keep you there.

A lot of people get fearful when they realise the enemy is out to get them. This is usually because they haven't got the revelation or certainty in their heart that God is more powerful and has already defeated the enemy.

You don't have to live a defeated life under the enemy, so here are a few things you should know about his boundaries:

No permission

The Word instructs us to be *aware* of the ways of the enemy:

> Be sober, be vigilant; because your adversary the devil walks about like a roaring lion, seeking whom he may devour.[7]

It stands to reason that if he is seeking whom he *may* devour, there are those he *may not* attack. Get committed to living your life in such a way that he may not devour you. He may try, but he won't be successful. Simply make the decision that he may not.

When Jesus confronted the demon-possessed man at Gadara, the demons began to beg and plead that He would permit them to go into the pigs. This is how it ought to be. Instead of begging the devil to leave you alone, he should be pleading with you to leave him alone.

Those demons had no more power than Jesus permitted them to have. As believers, we have been given that same authority. The enemy can only plunder where there is opportunity, so you have to decide that he *may not*!

No advantage

The devil will never play fair, so he'll take advantage of you whenever he can.

> For if indeed I have forgiven anything, I have forgiven that one for your sakes in the presence of Christ, lest Satan should take advantage of us; for we are not ignorant of his devices. [8]

If you are holding on to unforgiveness, bitterness or resentment, he will use those attitudes to bring destruction in your life. Don't be ignorant of the enemy's methods, or give him room to move. Bullet-proof your health, your marriage, your finances and your life by the Word of God.

No opportunity

If a man goes home every night and instead of communicating to his wife, he grunts at her, yells for the remote control and barks out orders, he is opening a door for the enemy to come in and plunder his marriage.

Wherever he has opportunity, the enemy will come in to wreak havoc. Remember that he can only succeed as far as you give him opportunity to do so. You need to make that decision: he *may not*!

No place

The Apostle Paul firmly instructs us:

> ... nor give place to the devil. [9]

Be wise to the devices and strategies of the enemy. If you leave him a gap, you can be sure he will take it. He will use anything that falls outside God's Word and principles. Paul knew how the enemy worked and urged us to deal with our attitudes to avoid giving him the opportunity to work.

It is rather like a game of tennis. If you kept playing from the net on one side, you'd be leaving the rest of the court wide open to your opponent's advantage. Don't give the enemy a wide open court, and make sure you cut off all the angles where he could take advantage of you.

By giving the enemy no room to move, you can avoid falling into his traps of destruction. This first step in getting out of a mess involves applying and building God's principles into your life. They form a hedge of protection that will safeguard you against the schemes of the enemy.

CHANGE
A MESS INTO A MESSAGE

CHAPTER FIVE

CHANGE
THE COURSE OF YOUR LIFE

Looking back at the course my life has taken so far encourages me and spurs me on. There have been numerous tests and trials along the way, but the triumphs and victories are awesome.

> When I hear somebody sigh "Life is hard" I am always tempted to ask, "Compared to what?" - Sydney Harris

When you are in the midst of a test or trial, it may seem as if life is an uphill climb, but we have been given godly principles that enable us to overcome any obstacle.

It doesn't mean that tests and trials won't come. For example, it is inevitable that at some stage you will be hurt and offended. This is what Jesus said:

> It is impossible that no offences should come, but woe to him through whom they do come! [10]

You cannot live your life without hurtful things happening, but some never recover from the hurt and pain they experience. They hold on to bitterness and offence, allowing it to rule them. Then they end up missing so much that God has in store for them.

The sad thing about people who get offended is that they inevitably find others who are nursing the same hurt and bitterness, and end up justifying their anger and offence. Consequently, they never see life differently.

> The difference between greatness and mediocrity is often how an individual views a mistake.
> – Nelson Boswell

Jesus had every reason to be offended; His disciples abandoned Him in His darkest hour, and Peter denied Him three times. But He understood the truth and wisdom of God's Word: that His Father would never leave Him nor forsake Him.

Along the journey of life, the crossroads of decision will set you on a course that will either have positive or negative consequence. Offence can be the beginning of a chain reaction of negative responses. Don't go down that road, and if you already have, turn back now. It leads only to destruction.

The victim mentality

First of all, when people find themselves in a negative situation, they generally start believing that they are the victim. They ask, "Why me? Why did God let this happen to me?" The moment they feel that there is no answer, the Bible says they open themselves up to depression and hopelessness.

> Anxiety in the heart of man causes depression. [11]

Depression produces that feeling of 'no way out', hope seems distant and they become sick on the inside. Instead of having resolve to change their circumstances and move on, people cave in, give up and develop the victim mentality. They give themselves a reason and excuse to stay where they are.

In later chapters, in order to move forward we will look at how to break the power of excuse in our lives.

Looking for sympathy

Once someone develops a victim mentality, the next step in the chain reaction is that they begin to draw close to others who can relate to their situation and sympathise with them. Sympathy is not always what one needs in this situation, because sympathy identifies with the problem or the hurt. Sympathy may make you feel a little better for a time, but it will not help you move forward.

Jesus was never moved by sympathy – but every time He was moved with compassion, something powerful happened. Sympathy doesn't have any answers, but compassion is a powerful force.

Unfortunately when one starts to see oneself as a victim, they feel the need to draw alongside others who think the same way. Be careful that you don't surround yourself with people who are going to hold you back. Rather position yourself in a challenging environment that will direct you towards answers.

One has to be very careful of going down this victim road as it has the potential to seriously sabotage your life. The enemy can (and will) take advantage, and may bring people into your life who will trap you into even more negative thinking.

We all want others to understand the reasons why we are hurt, but this can develop into dangerous thinking, which can carry a hefty price tag.

It then becomes your theology

The next step in the chain is that you begin to build this victim mentality into your theology by bringing what you believe down to your level of experience. Again, in the midst of the chain reaction, it is easy to begin to think "Well, this is my lot in life – this is what God wanted for me."

But look at the testimony of someone like David. He made mistakes, failed morally and was hunted down by Saul, yet he was still able to rise above all this and declare of the Lord:

> You are the portion of my inheritance and my cup. You maintain my lot. [12]

If God is maintaining and overseeing your lot in life, the story of your life is going to be a good one. David made many mistakes and experienced opposition from all sides throughout his life, yet he always saw the good side. For someone who wants to wallow in their misery and self-pity, the positive and optimistic attitude of people like David will annoy them.

Perhaps you know people like David - always optimistic about the future and no matter what they face, it always seems to work out well. If you desire to be such a person, it starts with the choice of changing your attitude in the midst of oppression. Refuse to be a victim!

CHANGE
THE COURSE OF YOUR LIFE

CHAPTER SIX

CHANGE YOUR EXPECTATIONS

God's plan and promise for us is that we are victorious, prosperous and blessed, across the entire spectrum of our lives. We will face tough times and obstacles, but instead of them knocking us down, we should emerge triumphant!

I have mentioned how the enemy is often the reason why some people constantly live in a mess, and another reason is people let hurt and offence dictate the course of their life.

Maybe these reasons are valid, but that won't change anything. Blaming the devil for all the bad things that have gone wrong in your life is sometimes easier than taking any *responsibility* yourself. The reality is that people don't like being accountable for their own actions.

Today you hear of lawsuits where one party sues another for negligence in an attempt to remove the blame from themselves. It is the natural instinct of the human race to justify their actions. Those who go into therapy may discover why they behave the way they do. While that's not necessarily a bad thing, blaming one's parents, one's background or one's experiences for the way they are, can give them a reason to *remain in that state*.

While the enemy is always intent on bringing chaos and calamity, he may not be completely responsible for the mess you may find yourself in. We often choose to ignore the signals or warnings that could prevent a chain of events that could eventually lead to a set of chaotic circumstances.

Most people with problems have a string of excuses or reasons to justify the way their lives are, but that will never allow them to move forward. By making yourself accountable, you build the foundation for the purposes of God to work in your life.

Instead of blaming circumstances or others, realise that you are accountable for your own life. When you give your life to Christ, the Bible says that old things pass away, and everything becomes new. If you become accountable, you will change the course of your life and begin to prosper.

> You never find yourself until you face the truth.
> – Pearl Bailey

Accountability begins with being honest about yourself and objective about situations. The decisions you make play a big part in creating the environment you find yourself in. Even the avoidance of a decision can trigger a string of unfortunate circumstances. In hindsight, you will possibly see that in many cases you would have had different and better results if *you* had made a different decision.

Be careful what you ignore

There is an old saying, 'ignorance is bliss,' but the reality is that ignoring or choosing to avoid certain fundamentals in life can result in messy or binding situations.

Don't ignore God's Word

The Bible is God's Word to us. It is not a set of rules or regulations, but is given to help and guide us through life. It releases and builds, and people tend to mess up their lives when they ignore what God says.

When it comes to relationships, don't ignore God's wisdom. If you become involved in moral impurity, it *will* (not might) hurt you. At the very least, it will cause a lot of pain and grief, and may even cost you a relationship that God intended to bless you with.

The Bible says that there is nothing new under the sun. It amazes me that some people think they are in a separate category to anyone else's situation and require special treatment. Even though there are case histories and overwhelming evidence of others who fell into the same trap, they ignore it. In an attempt to justify their actions and attitudes, they convince themselves that their circumstances are different, and as a result, nothing changes.

Choosing to live according to the principles of God is one of the greatest keys to changing any situation or circumstance. Look at this promise:

> So shall My word be that goes forth from My mouth; it shall not return to Me void, but it shall accomplish what I please, and it shall prosper in the thing for which I sent it. [13]

God always has our best interests at heart. You can stand on God's Word in confidence, knowing that what He said, He will do.

Don't ignore wise counsel from others

Who do you allow to speak into your life? In today's world, there is a vast array of voices all demanding your attention. Those who continually find themselves going through tests and trials in life are possibly listening to the wrong voices:

> Where no counsel is, the people fall: but in the multitude of counselors there is safety. [14]

We all need to have people whom we can trust and respect, who carry wise counsel. When it comes to making the major decisions for our church, I have a great team whose godly advice I respect.

Many people end up in a mess because they open themselves up to the opinions of *anyone* who will listen. You need to know where to go for wise counsel that will keep you on course. It is essential to align yourself with a network of strong Word-based Christians who can speak into your life. Many local churches have home fellowship groups in place for this very reason.

Those who choose to isolate themselves from such counsel often destine themselves for trouble.

On the other hand, too many counsellors can also set you on the road to difficulty. A 'multitude of counsellors' doesn't mean listening to the butcher, the baker and the candlestick maker. Or the hairdresser for that matter! (It's amazing the kind of conversations that take place in hair salons, and the advice that is freely given.)

The people who have been speaking into your life may not be bad people, but if their counsel is not based on the Word of God, you could find yourself making bad choices and wrong decisions.

Blessed is the man who walks not in the counsel of the ungodly.[15]

Make sure that the instruction you get lines up with the Word of God. If need be, change your 'therapist' and find those who will give you godly counsel for your situation. Open your life to people who can speak into your life, who can lift you up, who care about you and desire to see you released into what God has called you to do.

Don't ignore your instincts

Don't ignore your own better judgement. Your *conscience* is a gift from God and to a certain extent, you need to trust your common sense and judgement.

The saddest thing about common sense is that it is not very common. When you give your life to Christ and are filled with the Holy Spirit, you can rely on your instincts. I believe this is that 'still small voice' or the intuition people sense on the inside. Don't ignore it, but learn to listen to it and allow the outcome to be your judge.

Taking responsibility and making a firm decision about what you will allow to influence your life is a step in the right direction to setting the course of your life.

In the last three chapters, I've shown you how people get themselves into a mess – by giving the enemy room to move, by allowing a chain reaction of negative reactions and by ignoring wise counsel.

There is no excuse to stay in a mess, because God has equipped us with everything we need to change every test into a testimony and every trial in a triumph!

CHANGE YOUR EXPECTATIONS

PART 2

BREAK THE POWER OF EXCUSES

You may make mistakes, but you are not a failure until you start blaming someone else

(Anonymous)

CHAPTER SEVEN

CHANGE YOUR WAYS

As a young pastor I once took matters into my own hands. For a number of weeks, our church services had been plagued by a guy who was intent on creating havoc. He fooled around, and would occasionally light up a cigarette during services to draw attention to himself. He even attempted to sell drugs to new believers in the front of the building. When anyone tried to stop him, he would swear and curse at the top of his voice.

One Sunday, he went too far. He had had a fallout with an usher and was obviously looking for a fight. At the end of the service, as I was leaving the church, he grabbed me and pinned me against the wall, shouting abuse. I realised he was going to hit me, so I got in first. I punched him.

Well, he went down like a tonne of bricks – it was just like the movies! He began to scream at the top of his voice, "Pastor Brian hit me, Pastor Brian hit me" as our diligent ushers attempted to keep him quiet. They pushed me into the car, but as I began to drive away, he chased after us, kicking the car as he ran.

Doing things *my way* made good sense in that moment of madness. I stopped the car and chased him down the driveway, and we ending up wrestling on the side of the road. In the midst of it all, someone called the police.

I had just preached a lovely, uplifting sermon to the congregation, filling them with hope and answers, and then moments later, I was fighting outside the church building! While the police arrested and charged him with assault, I went home to spend the week in embarrassment. In one instant, I had allowed my flesh to take over and who knew what the consequences would be for our church? Who was going to turn up the next Sunday and listen to a pastor who resorted to brawling?

As it turned out, God's grace (and sense of humour) was greater. As I humbly apologised to our congregation for my behaviour, they stood up and applauded. Obviously they weren't condoning my actions, but they were standing by me as their pastor, warts and all. The thought did enter my head that perhaps this was a key to growing a church! (Just kidding!)

Admittedly I was a lot less mature then, but I learned a valuable lesson as a pastor of a growing church. Whenever I've tried to do things my way, I have made mistakes. I cannot indulge the thought of building the church *my* way – it has to be God's way.

The Bible says that unless the Lord builds the house, they labour in vain (Psalm 127:1). Now I leave it up to Him. The Lord's way is a higher way, and choosing to live His way opens up the promise of a life of blessing and destiny.

> 'For My thoughts are not your thoughts, nor are your ways My ways,' says the Lord. 'For as the heavens are higher than the earth, so are **My ways higher than your ways**, and My thoughts than your thoughts.' [16]

Which way are you living?

Frank Sinatra was applauded all over the world for his legendary song "I did it my way." It was a popular song that was cheered by many, but to be honest, it doesn't hold any powerful truths. In fact, doing things *your* way can lead to disaster.

If you want to change your future, you need to make a calculated decision about which way you want your life to go. There are those who live according to their own philosophies and belief systems, and while these may be based on good, moral principles, they still miss the fact that there is a higher (and better) way.

If you are living life your own way, it cannot produce the plan and destiny God has for you. There are a lot of people who go through the motions of the Christian life, but still live according to their way. Not surprisingly, they end up frustrated and confused because they aren't seeing the promises of God working in their life.

When you give your life to Christ, you make Him *Lord* of your life. That means you lay down your own way of living and choose His ways.

As you grow in God, you build on that foundation and live according to His principles and promises. His Word guides and directs you according to His ways. When you decide to do things your way, you are putting tremendous limitations in place because *your* way is not God's way. Not only is His way higher than our way, it comes with a guarantee. His way will never fail and will always result in fruitfulness and blessing.

There are those who embrace some of God's ways in their life and yet choose to ignore others. They are still trying to live life their own way, but you can't obey *some* of His commandments and expect to reap *all* of the blessing.

> There is a way that **seems** right to a man, but its end is the way of death. [17]

The scriptures speak of 'a' way, 'your' way and then God's way. There are many who live *a* way, which may not be necessarily bad or evil, but *a* way or *your* way has limitations and it will never be as powerful as God's way.

You can go a certain way on your own, but to say, "I did it my way" will seriously limit your life and hold you back from God's best. It is when you are honest enough to admit that your way isn't taking you where you long to go, and choose to live God's way that your life will begin to change.

CHANGE YOUR WAYS TO HIS WAY

CHAPTER EIGHT

CHANGE YOUR DECISION-MAKING PROCESS

People make all sorts of decisions regarding their life according to what *seems right*, and in doing so, deceive themselves into thinking that way *is right*.

For instance, a married man who begins to get closer to another woman will inevitably begin to entertain thoughts like "she understands me, but my wife doesn't." From there, he could begin to fantasise about how different his world would be with her. Giving the enemy opportunity to build on that, he creates a picture of what it *could be* like.

However, what doesn't come into the equation is the pain it will cause, the effect on his children and the wasted years rebuilding his life. He just sees a deceptive, appealing picture of someone who understands him, but it doesn't tell the whole story.

But each one is tempted when he is drawn away by his own desires and enticed.[18]

In the Greek, 'drawn away' means 'allurement' or 'deceitful representations.' That is exactly how the enemy works, only telling half the story and showing half the picture.

Those who backslide from God inevitably do so because they are drawn away by their own desires – either offences or hurt, or because they've allowed mediocrity to rule, or perhaps have given place to the power of sin.

Your own desires and ways will drag and tempt you away from God's purposes. The Word says that God won't tempt anyone beyond what they are able to bear, but temptation is all about being drawn away by one's *own desires* and filled with one's own way. That is when you begin to open yourself up to the pretty picture in your mind, not realising that it is a mirage and doesn't tell the whole story. Most of the time it is a lie, and so many people sabotage their own life according to such pictures.

Short-sighted decisions

You can make some foolish and short-sighted decisions by living according to what seems right. Look at what happened to Esau when he came in from a day of hunting and was incredibly hungry. He saw the stew that Jacob had cooked and his scale of measure became imbalanced. His tiredness and hunger rated a 'ten' while his birthright rated 'one.' His birthright was his destiny; it was his potential and everything God had in store for him as the oldest son, and he carelessly gave it up because of his temporary physical needs.

You can fall into the same trap when you major on minors and minor on the majors. People build their own reality according to what they experience in life. All some hear is negativity, and others only hear what they want to hear. It is from this standpoint that they determine how far they go in life. Jesus said:

> Take heed what you hear. With the same measure you use, it will be measured to you; and to you who hear, more will be given. [19]

You need to set your scale of measure according to the Word of God so that you will make good value judgements, and not abort your potential and God-given opportunities.

Of the huge crowd that gathered together on the Day of Pentecost, why did some embrace the outpouring of God, and others mock it? To those who place a higher value on the things of God, they will measure and receive it accordingly.

It even happens in church, where one person will leave a service excited about what they received from God, and another walks out glum-faced, having not received anything. It all depends on where that person's scale is set.

People end up making foolish decisions because what *seems right* to them is elevated to a position above God's way. You need to make sure that what seems right, *is* right!

Jesus said many amazing and powerful things, but in reality we find Christians who accept one thing and not another. There are those who believe that Jesus heals today but don't believe in tithing. Others who tithe and give regularly may reject water baptism or baptism of the Holy Spirit. You need to be open to the whole Word of God.

Another example is where Christians only see truth from one position or perspective. Jesus said:

> In the world you will have tribulation; but be of good cheer, I have overcome the world. [20]

Some will read that verse and only see, "you will have tribulation." They go on to build their understanding around a narrow, ominous, hopeless outlook. Then there will be those who gladly receive "but be of good cheer, I have overcome the world." They are full of optimism, but may get shocked and disillusioned when opposition comes their way.

Jesus made both statements, but each person has paid attention to only one aspect, according to their own mental scale. The result is that they may end up disillusioned and disappointed.

When something happens that contradicts what they believe, people get disillusioned with Christianity and think the Bible isn't valid. For instance, after much prayer and faith, someone may have a wonderful God-given opportunity to buy a beautiful new house. They will be rejoicing and praising Him because of this blessing in their life. But what happens if one week later the hot water cylinder breaks and the carpets are destroyed? Do they abandon their faith and feel disillusioned and disappointed with God?

I have often heard of those who make a commitment to the Lord suddenly having all hell break loose in their lives. That is no time to get disappointed, offended or disillusioned. Determine to stand on the Word and see the whole counsel of the Word of God work in your life. It is not about believing what you want to believe.

Make sure that what you hear lines up with the Word of God, and then align your decision-making process with what *is right*. If you don't, deception may enter the picture and God's purpose may be sabotaged.

CHANGE YOUR DECISION-MAKING PROCESS

CHAPTER NINE

CHANGE YOUR FOCUS

Human nature naturally leaps to shift focus and lay guilt, shame and excuse at someone else's feet.

After Adam and Eve had tasted the forbidden fruit in the Garden, God asked Adam if he had eaten from the tree. Adam had his excuse ready: "The *woman* whom You gave to be with me, she gave me of the tree, and I ate." He not only blamed his wife, but he even blamed God for giving her to him. Then God spoke to Eve, and she blamed the snake: "The *serpent* deceived me, and I ate."

Well, nothing has really changed. The instinct to shift blame to someone or something else has been passed on through the generations. Today you often hear people saying things like "Well, I can't change the way that I am because …" and they go on to list the reasons, or you have others who say "Well, it's different for me because …" and then demand to be excused because of their 'unique' situation. Then there are those who abdicate all responsibility and blame someone else, saying "it's just not my fault!"

> The reason people blame things on the previous generations is that there is only one other choice.
> – Doug Larson

Don't miss God's mark

Sin and excuse are closely linked. In ancient Greek, 'hamartia,' the word for sin, means 'to miss the mark.' Both *sin* and *feeble excuses* have the power to make you miss God's mark.

No matter what challenges are in front of you, God has set the mark. If you are committed to changing your future and living a life full of potential, you cannot justify staying where you are. You have to keep moving forward.

> I press toward the **mark** for the prize of the high calling of God in Christ Jesus.[21]

The 'mark' is all that is in Christ Jesus. We are called to be 'spiritual marksmen', aiming to hit the target and shatter the bull's-eye. That should be our goal.

There are those who try and adjust the mark to line up with their circumstances. They shoot their arrow and then paint the bull's-eye around it. Others aim at nothing and hit it every time.

An excuse mentality will always find reasons to justify why they cannot succeed. Yet our excuses don't cut it with God. Through the blood of Jesus Christ, our sins are forgiven and we have everything available to us to hit that mark.

The limitations of excuses

Excuses always limit potential and lull people into feeling better about not achieving God's mark. This mentality will prevent them moving forward.

Excuses enable you to turn back when the heat is on

Excuses are really an issue of the heart. When you are in the heat of battle, or in the midst of adversity, what is in your heart will be revealed.

> ... a generation that did not set its heart aright, and whose spirit was not faithful to God. The children of Ephraim, being armed and carrying bows, **turned back in the day of battle.**[22]

The children of Ephraim were a generation whose heart wasn't right. Even though they were armed and prepared for battle, they decided to turn back.

Turn up the heat in a marriage, and the typical response is to back away and blame your partner. We are armed with the Word of God, equipped for victory in every situation. If our hearts are right, we can apply His Word without an excuse or reason not to come through as overcomers in Christ.

Excuses mean you won't aim true

An excuse mentality can have you deceived about where the mark really is.

Watch out for this deception. Knowledge, understanding and wisdom are the three things that will keep you on track:

- Knowledge is the acquisition of facts and the truth,
- Understanding is the assimilation of facts and the truth, and
- Wisdom is acting on the facts and the truth.

Excuses will hinder prosperity

> He who covers his sins **will not** prosper, but whoever confesses and forsakes them will have mercy.[23]

The promise of God is for a life of abundance and prosperity in every area of life, so don't let excuses hold you back from hitting this mark.

Take up the challenge of building a great future according to the hope and promise of God, and aim for nothing less than the bull's-eye.

CHANGE YOUR FOCUS

CHAPTER TEN

CHANGE YOUR EXCUSES

Over the years I have listened with amusement to incredibly elaborate excuses my children have come up with to explain away some unfortunate event. As I listen to them, I realise that they have put a lot of creative thought and energy into their excuses. It's quite incredible what they come up with. Their excuses often remind me of the ones I used to make to my parents, which I thought were so convincing and totally believable.

The reality is that there is *no such thing as a good excuse*, yet we make them all the time. An excuse is the meat of a lie covered by the skin of a reason.

Don't justify an excuse mentality

When you listen to children making excuses, you begin to realise that adults aren't that different, except that they are more subtle in their justifications.

We live in an excuse-orientated society. People pay professionals hundreds of dollars to explain the way they are, and then use that counsel to justify their behaviour. It enables them to accept the way they are, without guilt. While some reasons may be legitimate and understandable, instead of accepting them and moving on, they use it as an excuse to continue living at that level.

If you want to change your future, you have to get rid of the excuses. There may be various reasons why you are the way you are, but no excuse is a good excuse.

Three typical excuses

In Luke chapter 14, Jesus told the story of the man who gave a great feast, and sent his servant to invite his guests. It tells how they all began to make excuses why they couldn't come.

God has extended an invitation to us all through the blood of Jesus Christ, and all we have to do is respond. Sadly, there are many who never enter the fullness of His blessing because they have an excuse for why they cannot.

This parable gives three common excuses and typical defences why so many don't enter God's purpose and destiny for their life.

1. Possessions

> The first said to him, 'I have bought a **piece of ground**, and I must go and see it. I ask you to have me excused.' [24]

This man had bought some land, and wanted to go and see it. If you have ever bought property, you will know how often you feel compelled to drive by and look at it. I know when I've been involved in building projects (either our own home or the church building) I find myself absorbed with watching the construction process, willing the workers on to make faster progress. During the first phase of our church building, no matter where I was going, I always found some reason to drive by the land.

There is nothing wrong with purchases and investments, but trouble begins when they become the pursuits that draw you away from the things of God.

No possession or investment, no matter how valuable it is, should ever draw us away from the purposes of God. Are your possessions a help or a hindrance to the cause of the Kingdom? This is often decided by your heart's attitude towards them. Do your possessions possess you?

The Word says that a 'rich man also will fade away in his pursuits' (James 1:11). Some have interpreted this as wealth being the cause of a rich man fading away. But it's not the issue of his wealth, as much as it is what he is pursuing.

Money with a Kingdom purpose isn't a problem, but be wary of possessions that can encumber and weigh you down. Instead of releasing you to fulfil His plan for your life, watch that finance and possessions don't become your excuse.

2. Business

> "And another said, `I have bought five **yoke of oxen**, and I am going to test them. I ask you to have me excused.'[25]

This man had bought some oxen, and his business interests were the basis of his excuse. Your vocation and career can become the excuse you use to miss the mark. Many people make the excuse "I can't come, I have to work." Extreme workaholics become obsessed with the pressure and commitments of their work, and ultimately it absorbs all their time and permeates every aspect of their life.

Now work itself isn't a problem. It is a biblical principle that "if you don't work, you don't eat." Check that your work lines up with the will of God, or whether you are moving the mark to suit your circumstances.

When you have a Kingdom spirit, your work will fall in line with the mark and the Word of God, presenting you with opportunity to use your God-given gifts and talents to build Kingdom finance into your life. Work isn't an excuse – it is what propels you and I into God's plan and purpose.

3. Relationships

> "Still another said, `I have married **a wife**, and therefore I cannot come."[26]

It is very sad when relationships become an excuse. Relationships are designed to be a blessing from God, and I know that I wouldn't be where I am today if it wasn't for my wife. We are a team in partnership together, aiming for God's ultimate in our lives.

When a spiritual leader abdicates his responsibilities or when one partner is regarded as an obstacle or a nuisance, this is when relationships begin to miss the mark. Conflict and tension is a result of people losing sight of the Cause of Christ, and it is often then that they move the mark for the sake of preserving the relationship.

Many try to separate and box the various aspects of their lives instead of letting them work together. Tension may build up when family time, church activities and God's time are regarded as isolated activities. These should all blend and flow, and it usually only requires a simple adjustment to one's thinking, to see them flowing together as one lifestyle.

Possessions, work and relationships are typical of most reasons people use today, but they are merely excuses preventing them from receiving God's blessing.

Excuses justify staying where one is at

Indulging excuses means you don't have to change or move on in life. All it does is justify your current lifestyle.

There are those who won't accept Jesus Christ as Lord of their lives because their excuse is that they aren't ready or good enough. The truth is that none of us will ever be ready or good enough. God's grace is the power of the New Covenant. It's got nothing to do with what we've done, but what Jesus has done for us. Excuses mean that you prefer your reasons for remaining static.

Excuses are self-focussed

All excuses justify 'me' and will usually be in the interests of self. The businessman, the property owner and the married man mentioned in the parable all gave their reasons for not attending the party. Their reasons all began with 'I'. Most excuses are inevitably self-absorbed.

Excuses validate mediocrity

No matter what challenges are before you, God has set the mark for your life. When people won't move past their excuses, He'll move on and use others instead.

The excuses made by the property-owner, the businessman and the married man in Luke 14 justified why they couldn't (or wouldn't) attend. Consequently, those invited to the party were the lame, the maimed and the blind.

I've noticed that many who succeed in life are not necessarily the most gifted, or talented, or the best at what they do. Instead, it is those who symbolically represent the lame, the maimed and the blind who have refused to live under the grip of an excuse-mentality, who receive the rewards.

Excuses champion a defeated outlook

When our children were growing up, we banned the phrase 'I can't' in our household. In the parable, the man with a wife explained, "...therefore I *cannot* come" but the reality was he *would not*. Declaring that you cannot do something means you are succumbing to a position of defeat before you even start.

Excuses are the language of victims

An excuse is to say, "It's not my fault" and is a statement looking for justification. The married man in the parable was behaving like a victim of some awful disease. He had just gotten married, and marriage should be one of the most wonderful experiences in life. Any relationship built around the Cause of Christ will bring freedom and release. It is when one's attention shifts from the Cause that marriage becomes a distraction.

Excuses breed a culture of hopelessness

Behaviour impacts our environment and creates a certain culture. In Luke 14, it described how "they *all with one accord* began to make excuses" (verse 18). If we are continually excuse-minded, that will spread quickly and the result will be excuses on every side, resulting in corporate mediocrity.

Excuses put success out of reach

The final outcome of the great feast in Luke 14 was that none of those men who were invited tasted the supper (verse 24). The consequence of their excuses was that success and accomplishment was far removed from them.

No matter what they are, excuses will ultimately rob you from fulfilling your potential in God. Instead of allowing the key areas of your life to justify missing the mark, line up your possessions, your career and your relationships according to the will of God and begin to move forward.

CHANGE YOUR EXCUSES IN LIFE

CHAPTER ELEVEN

CHANGE YOUR EXCUSE NATURE

While working on a series of teachings I did which I called 'Excuse me!' I began to notice how often I would use 'but' or 'because' to explain away circumstances. It is easy to spot someone else rationalising and justifying their errors, but when you start to see it in yourself, you are challenged to change.

As mentioned previously, the sin nature inherent in man causes us to instinctively leap at justifying our actions and cast blame on others.

What Jesus Christ accomplished on the cross reversed that 'curse.' Through Him, we are able to have an intimate relationship with God and have available to us all the resource to live our lives according to our full potential. The Word clearly instructs us how to overcome the negative effects of our excuse-orientated sin nature.

Transparency

O Lord, You have searched me and known me. [27]

The heart of David was transparent. He made plenty of mistakes, but throughout the Psalms you can see his openness and honesty in his relationship with the Lord.

Admitting mistakes and failures is hard for most human beings. An honest confession that simply says "I blew it" without making numerous excuses, is a rare occurrence.

I have often been in the situation where I've had to deal with the moral failure of people. It is very rare to hear anybody simply say, "I was wrong!" Even if there is partial acceptance of responsibility, human nature usually kicks in and begins to justify itself.

"*If* only my wife had been more understanding ...", or

"I want to rebuild my life *but* if there were only people to support me ...",

What is wrong with a good old-fashioned, "I was wrong, and I'm sorry?" That honesty and transparency is the starting point in the process of turning your life around. Such a confession and acknowledgement allows repentance, restoration and renewal to work. If you never get to that point, the ability to come back is limited. As some Bible heroes proved, there is life (and success) after tragedy and failure.

People want to look externally for reasons to justify situations, but God looks internally for *honesty*.

> For the Lord does not see as man sees; for man looks at the outward appearance, but the Lord looks at the heart. [28]

Human nature is always noticing the external, outward appearances, but God goes below the surface to identify the issues of the heart and the inner man.

While you shouldn't feel condemned by your natural responses, you can begin to become more internally focussed by taking on God's ways. An internalist will always ask, "What can I learn from this and what can I do to change?"

If you are determined to change the future, it may require stopping long enough to address those issues in your life that will hinder God's plan and potential for your life. Being open and transparent is the first step towards overcoming the excuse nature.

Accountability

So then each of us shall give account of himself to God. [29]

Developing a spirit of accountability will keep you on course. Many excuses and reasons may be valid, but in the long run, when you stand in front of the Lord, it will sound petty and feeble to keep bringing up what someone else did or how you felt in the midst of a lame excuse.

Many years ago, I got annoyed when our council workers refused to empty our garbage bin one day. They put a large sticker on the bin which said 'too heavy!' I was prepared to take it further, by writing a letter of complaint to the council. The truth was, the bin was full of gravel (and too heavy!) Imagine me, standing before the Lord giving account of my actions, justifying my behaviour by saying, "So what was I supposed to do with my gravel?"

We have to learn accountability, to take responsibility when it is due. Many people neglect this because they are so pre-occupied with keeping accounts. Their memory stores up hurt, injustice, attack and persecution. Suppress these things long enough and they will become a volcano waiting to erupt.

While David was king of Israel, there was a famine in the land (2 Samuel 21). When David asked God why there was a famine, the Lord explained it was because Saul and his armies had killed the Gibeonites. David could have settled for that as his excuse to justify the famine, but he went one step further. He took accountability and attempted to change the situation by calling in the Gibeonites and asking what he could do for them to make amends.

If you want to be free from a situation, it may mean rectifying something that wasn't even your doing. Build the kind of spirit that says, "what can *I* do to make things right?'

and you will begin to live free from the consequences of the sin nature.

Confession

> Repent therefore and be converted, that your sins may be blotted out, so that times of refreshing may come from the presence of the Lord. [30]

True confession has no hidden agendas. Jesus described the prayers of two different men:

> Two men went up to the temple to pray, one a Pharisee and the other a tax collector. The Pharisee stood and prayed thus with himself, 'God, I thank You that I am not like other men—extortioners, unjust, adulterers, or even as this tax collector. I fast twice a week; I give tithes of all that I possess.' And the tax collector, standing afar off, would not so much as raise his eyes to heaven, but beat his breast, saying, 'God, be merciful to me a sinner!' [31]

The first one tried to impress God, highlighting his own goodness by pointing out the sins of everyone else. The second man was open and transparent in his humility and repentance. His confession came from the heart.

In order to live free, we need to confess what needs to be confessed, instead of drawing back to lick our wounds. Confession, grace and mercy provide for our redemption, and enable us to live with a free Christ-like nature.

CHANGE YOUR EXCUSE NATURE

PART THREE

CHANGE
THE POWER
OF THE PAST

**To design the future effectively,
you must first let go of your past**

(Charles J. Givens)

CHAPTER TWELVE

CHANGE
THE POWER OF SECRECY

The world media went into a frenzy when the South African cricket captain, Hansie Cronje, admitted that he had been corrupted by an Indian bookmaker. He was highly respected as a role model in his own nation and in other cricket-playing nations. What was done in secret was broadcast across the earth.

It was a sad day for South Africa and world-wide cricket when he telephoned my good friend, Ray McCauley in the early hours of the morning to confess. As the story unfolded, it became even more tragic and everything he had built in his life that far was now destroyed by his secrecy.

If you want to change your future, you will need to check if there are any skeletons lurking in your closet. While there are things you don't know about me, and things I don't know about you, God is intimately acquainted with all our ways. We cannot hide from Him because He knows our thoughts, the issues of our heart, and what goes on in the inner man.

> For God will bring every work into judgement, including **every secret thing**, whether good or evil. [32]

Some people are held back and bound by secrets that hold them captive. While secrecy within your intimate relationships is a blessing, there is a perverted form of secrecy that can be destructive. People develop a secretive nature which makes them aloof, defensive or protective, and invariably builds walls around them.

God is not out to embarrass or humiliate anyone, but He does allow dark secrets to be exposed to the light, in order to release people into the fullness of His blessing. He is described as 'the God of gods, the Lord of kings, and a *revealer of secrets*' (Daniel 2:47).

The power of secrecy

The power of secrecy relates to those intimate and private aspects of our lives, that may include relationships, financial dealings, thoughts, attitudes and actions. It is these areas that may be unseen to the majority, but have enormous power when it comes to our future.

The Secret Place

God's domain is the secret place. Psalm 91 describes dwelling in the "*secret place* of the Most High." In Matthew 6, Jesus spoke about praying to our Father "who is in the *secret place*."

It is God's will for us to have an intimate relationship with Him. Through prayer and worship, as well as reading His Word, we build that intimacy into our lives. The secret place is essential in cultivating the powerful purposes of God, however your relationship with God should never be a secret.

You cannot be a closet Christian and then expect God's power to work openly and effectively in your life. This is why people are encouraged to publicly go forward to the altar to give their lives to Christ, or be baptised in water in a public ceremony.

> For I am not ashamed of the Gospel of Christ, for it is the power of God to salvation for everyone who believes. [33]

There should be no shame in telling people you are a

Christian. It is your declaration of your relationship with God that gives it *power*!

Some intimacies should never be a secret

The marriage ceremony is generally a very public event, even though the intimacies within the marriage are private. Standing before witnesses and making vows in the company of people to 'love, honour and cherish, in sickness and in health, for richer or for poorer,' you are reinforcing your commitment to that relationship. Eloping may sound like a spontaneous, fun idea to some, but there is an element of secrecy to it that can weaken the relationship.

Something significant and powerful happens when a relationship is declared publicly. There is a degree of privacy within every intimate relationship, but some intimacies should never be kept secret. Intimate relationships that are formed outside the context of a marriage union have the potential to bring destruction and pain. Many have been caught out for not being honest about improper relationships that exist in secret.

A basic rule to follow is that if you can't declare it publicly, you shouldn't have it. Instead of empowering you, it imprisons you when you aren't open, honest and transparent about it.

Secrecy has the potential for good and evil

If some secrets will empower you and others will bind and render you powerless, how do you know the difference? The measure is simple:

> ... in the day when God will judge the secrets of men by Jesus Christ, according to my Gospel. [34]

You need to ask yourself if your secret lines up with the Word of God. Does it bring shame, and can it hurt other people? Does it involve deception or does your secret exist because of guilt?

The Gospel deals with everything that has the potential to

imprison and bind you. The Word teaches us to bring all things into the light, opening up to God and to others. Even though He knows your intimate secrets, by opening your life up to Jesus, you enable Him to break the power of destructive secrets.

Exposing secrets to the light

While you first need to expose your life to Christ, there are times when you may be required to reveal secrets to others in order to be free from them.

> For nothing is **secret** that will not be revealed, nor anything hidden that will not be known and come to light.[35]

Jesus is the Light, so that's where our confession rests. Whether we need to tell any other people is another issue. To discern whether you should tell others, ask yourself the following questions and truthfully answer them.

Can you leave it behind and break its hold without telling anyone?

Eating disorders are often disguised with deceptive behaviour. Sometimes you may need to find a godly confidante who can have input into your life and help you remain free of that secretive activity.

Is it genuinely dead?

Be aware that something lying dormant may not necessarily be dead. Don't assume that you won't be tempted further down the line. Weigh up the consequences if it resurrected itself in your life. It may be wiser to inform and be accountable to others.

Is it already covered by grace?

The heart of God is to see you set free, and the grace of God is all sufficient, covering a multitude of sins. He is a loving, merciful God with your interests at heart. For your own sake, His love and grace will cover you *for a season*, giving you the opportunity to put your life right.

For the sake of the people you love, the grace of God can protect them from the hurt and pain your secrets may cause. Know that God believes in you and His desire is to see you set free to fulfil the great plans and purpose He has for your life.

Is it going to catch up with you anyway?

Will your secret catch up with you and trip you up at a later stage? You need to address the secrets that could bring destruction in the future.

> As a partridge that broods but does not hatch, so is he who gets riches, but not by right; It will leave him in the midst of his days, and at his end he will be a fool. [36]

If your life is built on a foundation of dishonest dealings from your past, you will reap the consequences somewhere down the line. Make the choice to put them behind you, expose them to the light and move forward.

If you feel you have dealt with the issue and it is genuinely dead, and won't cause any unnecessary hurt, then perhaps there is no reason to tell anyone. For instance, a woman who had a secret abortion twenty years ago, who has repented and received forgiveness and healing from the Lord, may not need to tell others. The real question is whether that secret is still keeping her bound and unable to move on.

> Bring my soul out of prison, that I may praise Your name. [37]

Don't harbour secrets that may hold you back and imprison you. Wipe the slate clean once and for all, and move forward into the amazing future God has in store for you.

CHANGE
THE POWER OF SECRECY

CHAPTER THIRTEEN

CHANGE THROUGH REPENTANCE

Everyone can experience moments of embarrassment, or have actions or situations that they regret. The mind has the incredible ability to replay the events of the past over and over again, but the good news is that no matter what happened in the past, it cannot affect your future ... unless *you* of course allow it to.

Many people get stuck in the past and cannot let go of what happened months or years ago. It hinders them from moving forwards, and holds them back from what God has in store for their lives. If you deal with it today, your future can be free.

> The past, though it cannot be relived, can always be repaired.
> – John La Farge

God still has a great plan for you, in spite of what may have happened. Repentance is a great starting point – everyone can make foolish decisions and mistakes, but repentance enables us all to move on, free of shame and regret.

Know the power of repentance

To repent means to turn around 180 degrees. Being truly repentant means you don't look for excuses. It means you are genuinely sorry for any actions and attitudes that have put you where you are. Above all, repentance means turning to God, literally throwing yourself on His mercy, and positioning yourself where He can pick you up and put you back on course.

Not only do we live life according to our *actions*, but we also live according to our *reactions*. Your attitude and thinking plays a very key role in determining what happens in your life.

Some people become highly defensive when it is suggested that they need to repent, and claim that the mess they are in is an undeserved attack of the devil. Now perhaps the enemy did bring an attack, but we need to make sure that our hearts remain pure and correct. If you are unfairly hurt by another's spiteful actions, but you hold bitterness and offence in your heart against them, *you* will need to repent and ask God's forgiveness. It is the attitude, not the action, that can keep you from moving forward.

Motivational courses, visits to a counsellor, even frequent trips down to the altar don't necessarily facilitate change. Change begins with an internal decision to turn around and turn away from whatever is holding you bound.

Changing house, changing cars, changing jobs or church (or even changing a marriage partner) won't help the long-term problem.

To repent is a decisive commitment that allows God to change you on the inside. It affects your heart, your attitudes and your behaviour. It is a commitment to accept the grace of God.

Accept God's grace

You can sing "Amazing Grace" till the cows come home and never actually become a recipient of it. Grace finds its purpose on a foundation of repentance and accountability, and the power of grace is weakened when those foundations aren't addressed. Justifying, making excuses and blaming others never allows grace to be released.

When you accept Christ, your sins are blotted out. You may pride yourself on having a long memory, but when it comes to sin, God has a wonderful 'forgettery.' Once you have repented and received forgiveness, He wipes the slate clean for you to begin again. This is a supernatural event, and can literally destroy the power of natural events that took place. In other words, your hurt and pain can be completely reversed through the power of His grace.

Far too many Christians allow their memories to keep them prisoner to their past sins, which in turn hold them in condemnation. You need to see yourself the way Christ sees you. If you really want to move on in life, you need to accept what Christ has done for you. Christ's undeserved grace begins as a spiritual work, but you need a commitment to endurance and perseverance to see the work completed.

Once you have repented and received forgiveness, you will feel a sense of peace and relief, but this may not happen immediately if you have woven yourself into a web. Of course God will instantly heal you spiritually, but you may have to work your way through some of the issues. Take a bank robber, for example, who accepts Christ as Lord of his life. Spiritually he is saved and cleansed, but he will still have to reap the consequences of what he has sown, and probably have to serve his prison term.

If you have been hurt and burned, it will take time to heal and recover from the effects of the heat. Embrace endurance and patience to hold on. Remain focussed and do not quit. Don't change your theology and belief system according to the level of your experience or what you are feeling.

It is God's will that you are healthy, whole and renewed but you have to make this commitment to endure and hold on. The presence of the Lord brings relief in the midst of tough times, resulting in recovery and positive change. By holding on to the promises of the Word in faith, you can leave the mess of the past behind and build a new life with a new beginning.

Don't fall back on old habits, old patterns and old thinking just because you do not think it is happening fast enough. Be determined to endure, and refuse to get caught up in the things that have previously ruled and bound you.

The past cannot shape your future if you don't allow it to. Examine yourself and ask God to show you the areas where you need to repent. The element of repentance is *not optional* if you want to deal with your past.

CHANGE
BY THE POWER OF REPENTANCE

CHAPTER FOURTEEN

CHANGE A CURSE INTO A BLESSING

When my father gave his life to Christ in 1940, he cut off the past and changed the future forever as he began to walk in the inheritance and blessing of God.

God's eternal plans go from generation to generation. While certain types of sin can run through generations, such as alcoholism, depression and divorce, you can cut off those *inherited* curses through the promise and power of God:

> Therefore, if anyone is in Christ, he is a new creation; old things have passed away; behold, all things have become new.[38]

From the moment you receive Christ in your life, old things are passed away and a new day dawns for the generations to come. The decisions you make have long-reaching consequences, firstly in terms of your own life and secondly, in how you affect others.

In the same way that generational curses get passed down as a heritage through families, so does generational blessing. If you are building your life based on God's Word and His blessing, you are building a great heritage for the generations to come. Look at how the Word describes the blessing of a righteous man:

> Blessed is the man who fears the Lord, who delights greatly in His commandments. His descendants will be **mighty** on earth; the generation of the upright will be **blessed**. **Wealth and riches** will be in his house, and his righteousness endures forever. Unto the upright there arises light in the darkness; he is gracious, and full of compassion, and righteous. A good man deals graciously and lends; he will guide his affairs with discretion.[39]

It talks about the descendants and generation of a righteous man. The Living Bible translates it that *a good man's sons have a special heritage*. And what a wonderful heritage it is! It includes prosperity and godly characteristics.

Now what if your parents weren't godly? Of course you would need to love and honour them as your parents, but you have the opportunity to build a new generation, *starting with you*. You can cut off the past and start anew.

A child who has suffered abuse is not doomed. If they grow up full of anger, bitterness and resentment, and never deal with the issues of the past, then they will never walk in their full God-given potential. But Christ can set them free from these curses of the past.

This change begins with *you*, once you get a revelation of who you are in Christ. You may look back through your family tree and see a recurring pattern: alcoholism, adultery, depression, gambling, suicide … but you don't have to be ruled by these things. Even though these tragedies may have passed through many generations, it can all turn around when it comes to you, because you are a new creation in Christ.

Changing the generations

When someone accepts Jesus, no matter who their parents were or what their background was, a *new heritage* begins.

Take the time to do an interesting comparison between the

good character of the righteous man in Psalm 112, with the attributes of God, described in the previous Psalm (Psalm 111). You'll find the wording is identical. The reason we can change the future is because our heritage is now linked to the nature and character of God the Father, rather than our parents or ancestors, whose natures are flawed.

> Train up a child in the way he should go, and when he is old he will not depart from it. [40]

From generation to generation, the goal is to build righteous principles (and therefore foundations) into our children. I look at young people in the church today and observe how they are becoming stronger, more confident and more able to express themselves clearly. I am several inches taller than my father, but my eldest son – at six feet, four inches – is taller than me. Not only are the generations getting bigger, but with Kingdom principles at *work* in their lives, the generations are getting stronger.

Sadly, the negative of this scripture also applies. If you train up children in negative ways, they may not depart from them either. You may hear a youngster vowing that he will never drink like his alcoholic father and another declaring she will never shout like her mother, but the tragedy is that people so often take on the very thing they despise. The reason is they have been trained in a certain way and they are candidates to be prisoners to it.

> Children have never been very good at listening to their elders, but they have never failed to imitate them.
> – James Balwin

The way you *think* is also passed down through generations. It amazes me how many Christians feel uncomfortable about the subject of wealth. Many people have grown up amid a battler mentality and cannot comprehend anything other than struggling financially. They would very likely feel guilty if they did have any money and would either justify it or hide it, rather than use it as an awesome tool for the Kingdom.

Christians have to change much of the thinking that has been passed down. It does nothing but limit and hold them back.

As you bring God into the picture, not only your life, but your descendants' lives will change. Cut off the old, break free of the curse and live in God's grace.

In the book of Ecclesiastes, King Solomon reflected on the futility and emptiness of life *without God*. Bring God into the picture and everything changes. By keeping His commandments, you will see the difference He makes, cutting off things that have affected and bound people for generations.

Take the Word of God, apply it and see its effect reach into future generations. There is a new hope and a new destiny.

CHANGE
A CURSE INTO A BLESSING

CHAPTER FIFTEEN

CHANGE THE PARENTING PROCESS

Have you ever watched spectators at a tennis match? Their heads go from side to side, following the action. As a boy, I would watch table tennis games with an open mouth and this earned me the nickname 'Fish.'

Recently I was watching my son play the bass guitar during a rehearsal with the youth band, and was amused to see a familiar blank expression on his face. There are some things that are definitely passed down from father to son ... and that's probably why my sons are so good looking!!

Today, there is a trend that targets one's father (or mother) as the source of blame for the way their lives have turned out. There is no parent on the entire planet who has never made a mistake in their parenting, but is it an acceptable excuse in the eyes of God to blame your parents for the way your life turns out?

Your father's fault?

There are those who carry major issues in life that relate directly to their father, or parents. Certain counselling enables them to justify their consequent behaviour, however, the Bible is a book of life and promise. While blessing and curses can be passed down through the generations, through the blood of Jesus Christ, we now live under a new covenant.

> What do you mean when you use this proverb concerning the land of Israel, saying: `The fathers have eaten sour grapes, and the children's teeth are set on edge?'[41]

The 'sour grapes' may refer to an austere father – one who didn't know how to give or to receive love, or one who was often absent or overly critical, or told his children they were never good enough. The 'teeth set on edge' talks about the bitterness and resentment it produces in their children.

As our society faces the ever-increasing breakdown of family, it is proven that the *role of the father* is highly significant. The impact and influence of parents is essential in the healthy shaping of children's lives, with undealt childhood dysfunctions becoming more prominent with age.

Deep feelings of insignificance, demotivation, resentment, rebellion and depression are often related to poor parental relationships. Devastated self-worth, rejection and even confused sexuality may result. Children who grew up hearing, "You're hopeless" or "You'll never amount to anything" inevitably tend to believe it. Ultimately the same dysfunctions are passed on through the generations, and one tends to see whole families with similar traits.

Free from blame

The good news is that the power of the generations is broken in the New Covenant. While the proverb stated the fathers had eaten sour grapes and the children's teeth were set on edge, the Lord declared that it would no longer be applicable. That portion of scripture goes on to state that in the Kingdom of God, fathers are not accountable for the sins of their children, nor children for the sins of their fathers.

> The soul who sins shall die. The son shall not bear the guilt of the father, nor the father bear the guilt of the son.[42]

Many Christians live their lives in condemnation because of mistakes and issues relating to their parents, but the Word declares one is no longer ruled by the sins of their fathers. The truth sets you free, and even if your father wasn't a godly man, *you* have a great inheritance in Father God. Read Psalm 112 again where it describes how the descendants of a good man have a special heritage, and will be honoured on the earth. That's God's promise to you!

Don't live according to the limitations of your natural parenting when you can have all the benefits of your heavenly Father. As you begin to see who Christ is in you, and who you are in Him, you will begin to become all He has called you to be.

Wise parenting

> The family you come from isn't as important as the family you are going to have.   – Ring Lardner

No matter what your upbringing was, you can change the future generations by becoming a wise and godly parent to your children. Proverbs 29 gives some excellent keys and wisdom to impact the future generations.

Don't be afraid of godly discipline

> Discipline your son, and he will give you peace; he will bring delight to your soul. (Verse 17)

The key to discipline is consistency. Never lose your temper and lash out. The emphasis is *godly discipline*, which is firm, unwavering, loving and righteous. Consistent discipline always produces great children.

Fill their lives with vision

> Where there is no vision, the people cast off restraint.
> (Verse 18a)

You cannot ignore the link between rebellion and lack of vision. Without vision, there is a sense of hopelessness and people will live carelessly. When you fill your children's lives with vision and purpose, they will have direction.

Keep the Word

> Blessed is he who keeps the Word. (Verse 18b).

When you train up children in the way they should go, they won't depart from it. Teaching them the principles of God and how to live life according to the Word will keep them on course.

Never underestimate the importance of example

> A servant cannot be corrected by mere words; though he understands, he will not respond. (Verse 19)

Basically, it's not what you say, but what you *do*, and who you *are* that will make the difference. Live as a godly example and your children will follow.

Your words have great power

> Do you see a man who speaks in haste? There is more hope for a fool than for him. (Verse 20)

The way you speak is powerful. By speaking negatively or by quickly losing your temper, you will influence your children. In the same way, positive words of life will impact their lives.

Love them, but don't spoil them

> If a man pampers his servant from youth, he will bring grief in the end. (Verse 21)

There is a vast difference between showing love and spoiling your children. My wife's father always said, "You can spoil your children as long as you spoil them with love."

Take responsibility for a peaceful home

> An angry man stirs up dissension, and a hot-tempered one commits many sins. (Verse 22)

Bring peace into your home by maintaining an even temper

and disposition. Learn not to "sweat the small stuff" and that unrighteous anger is a sin.

Be humble

> A man's pride brings him low, but a man of lowly spirit gains honour. (Verse 23)

Watch out for the destruction that comes with pride. A spirit of humility takes you much further in life than a spirit of pride. It is always a difficult lesson, but learn how to apologise. It's worth being transparent and honest at all times. And don't forget that the Word says that God resists the proud.

Ultimately you cannot go through life blaming your parents. No matter what your own personal experiences or relationship with your father or mother may have been, you can rise up and move forward. Breaking the power of the past will require commitment, but future generations will thank you for your courage.

CHANGE
THE PARENTING PROCESS

PART FOUR

CHANGE THE POWER OF TODAY

**A single day is enough to
make us a little larger,
or another time, a little smaller**

(Paul Klee)

CHAPTER SIXTEEN

CHANGE YOUR FUTURE – DAY BY DAY

What are the three most important days in your life? The first one is the day you were born. The second is the day you realised what you were born for, and the third is **today**, because today is really the only day that you have any power over.

If you want to change your future, you have to begin to realise the power that is in each individual day. Have you ever inquired of someone to hear them respond, "Oh, it's just *not my day?*" Well, the reality is, *it is our day*! It is a gift from God, and is full of potential and opportunity. You will never begin to positively change the future if you cannot address the everyday issues of life and initiate change there.

In seeing the significance of each day, you will begin to approach your future with a heart of wisdom. Don't take your days for granted; each one is specifically ordained by God and given to you as a gift.

Begin by numbering your days

One day when I was reading Psalm 90, all of a sudden a verse jumped out and challenged me:

So teach us to **number our days**, that we may gain a heart of wisdom.[43]

So that's what I did. That night I sat down with a pen and paper, and numbered my days. If it was going to help me get a *heart of wisdom*, I was happy to do it.

I started at the beginning of my life, on the day I was born (17 February, 1954), and wrote down: 'Day Number One'. Then I began to think of some of the more momentous days in my life and wrote them down too.

Day Number 1,826: Started school

Day Number 6,560: Bible College

Day Number 8,403: Wedding day (what a great day that was!)

Day Number 8,759: Moved to Australia from New Zealand

There were many other significant days I remembered, including the days our children were born and the day we first started our church in Sydney. I'll never forget the sense of elation as I ran toward my car at St Margaret's Hospital in Sydney after the birth of my first son. Or the pink banner declaring 'It's a girl!' erected above the church platform with accompanying pink balloons, to celebrate the birth of our daughter, Laura.

Doing a simple exercise like this can put life in perspective with a few strokes of the pen. In fact, life begins to look incredibly short when you list your days like this. But this is where a heart of wisdom begins.

Recognise whose day it is anyway

This is the day the Lord has made; we will rejoice and be glad in it.[44]

God made the day and gave it to us. In Genesis chapter one, it describes how He handcrafted the earth and called the light 'day.' The entire universe was put into place and time set in motion when He spoke it into being.

In a way, our days are not technically 'ours' because they all belong to Him. We talk about 'my day' and demand 'my time' or 'my space' but we are actually stewards over *His* day. Our days are given to us to serve Him, and we are accountable for what we do in our span of days. This doesn't mean we have to strive or work harder, but we should fill our days with all the life we can pack into them.

"*This* is the day that the Lord has made" – it doesn't focus on yesterday, tomorrow or the future, but it makes us look at what we have power over today. The Word doesn't say that if it is a good day we should rejoice. It challenges us to rejoice and be glad today, no matter what!

God has allotted a certain number of days to every one of us, and we need to make every one of them count. Don't get up in the morning and take the day for granted. You have to live every day wisely in order to be all that God has called you to be.

CHANGE YOUR LIFE – DAY BY DAY

CHAPTER SEVENTEEN

CHANGE YOUR ATTITUDE TOWARDS TODAY

I must confess that I love life. I've never been in a particular hurry for a Rapture because I want to live my life to the full. Don't settle for a mediocre life where one day runs into the next, where you just live out a bland Christian experience. There is so much more!

Instead of letting your days slip by aimlessly, recognise that every day is a gift from God, and desire to make every single one count. Once you realise the potential of every day, you will begin to approach them all wisely.

Make every day count

While the total number of our allotted days differs, there are some common aspects to each day. God has been fair in dealing us all an equal measure.

Every day has external influences

I remember one very disappointing day. It was my wife Bobbie's 40th birthday, and I went all out to make it a special event. (This was mainly because I messed up organising her 21st birthday, but that's another story.)

I arranged a stretch limo to take her for some beauty treatments in the city, and while she was away, I had a marquee set up, strung fairy lights in all the trees, called in the caterers and even had an orchestra. It was absolutely perfect ... except that it poured with rain. Of all the days I needed fine weather, it had to rain on that one!

The weather is one of those external influences that are beyond our control, but don't allow the weather to affect your day. Horrible weather doesn't mean it is a horrible day. As much as I love summer and warm, sunny weather, it is *not* the weather that determines the power of my day.

Every day has unpredictable circumstances

Besides the weather, all sorts of other unpredictable situations can happen in a day. After an exceptionally busy Friday which was jam-packed with meetings and functions, I got home relatively late that night looking forward to a good night's sleep.

I walked in to discover that my son had met with an unfortunate accident, and the next few hours were involved with assessing the extent of his injuries and getting him some medical attention. Not what I'd expected or planned, but the fact is that every day can throw up heaven's surprises or hell's invasions. There are things that you don't expect or deserve, but you end up dealing with them anyway. The Word wisely cautions us:

> Do not boast about tomorrow, for you do not know what a day may bring forth. [45]

Every day has 24 hours

"I wish I had more hours in the day!" I've said that before, and I'm sure you have too. But have you ever thought that someone like Richard Branson or Bill Gates has no more hours in their day than you do? No-one has more (or less) time than you have. It is dealt out equally to every one of us. We all have an equal measure.

Every person's day consists of *24 hours* – this same gift of 24 hours has been allocated to each of us, and it is up to us as individuals to make it count.

The power of a single day

When I numbered my days, I was surprised that I could only recall and account for about 200 major occasions.

To be honest, there are a lot of days that we can't even remember. Recently someone asked me, "Remember that time we went out to a dinner and you had Italian sausage?" They knew exactly what I ate, but I didn't even remember being there! Life can be a little like that.

While contemplating these inexplicable days, I discovered the answer in the Bible:

> The sun also rises, and the sun goes down, and hastens to the place where it arose. [46]

Solomon, in all his wisdom, realised a very simple yet powerful truth: the sun goes up and the sun goes down, and then goes back to start all over again. For some people, this is the entire quality of their life – the sun rising and the sun setting, day in and day out.

Well, that has happened over 16,800 times in my life (so far) – the sun has gone up and the sun has gone down. Ultimately that is what happened to those uneventful days I can't recall. But this doesn't mean those days were irrelevant. In fact, the opposite is true.

The way you approach all these 'normal' days determines the quality of your life. The substance of your life is not necessarily built on the big, momentous occasions. It is built rather on these ordinary days that we sometimes can't even remember. The principle is found in Zechariah 3:10: "For who has despised the day of small things?"

The day of small things is all about being consistent and faithful in the small things, including those seemingly insignificant days.

When Bill Clinton was inaugurated as the president of the USA, he became the most powerful man in the land. That must have been a big day in his life. Yet when Time magazine did a survey, asking what Bill Clinton would be most remembered for, only 17% said he would be remembered for the job he did as president. The great majority said he would mainly be remembered for the controversies in his personal life. Sadly, his approach to the 'minor' days in his life has marred his reputation.

Many people do not achieve their potential because of how they approach their days. Every day has great power in your life. If you can build the right kind of days, you can build a strong foundation for the future. No matter how long you have been on this earth, you are moving forward towards eternity and the end of your life.

Even though each day will come and go quickly, they are all ordained by God. I have purposed to make every day count, and to live each one to the maximum potential to which God has called me. By building the right kind of days, you can build the right tomorrows.

CHANGE YOUR ATTITUDE TOWARDS TODAY

CHAPTER EIGHTEEN

CHANGE
THE QUALITY OF EACH DAY

I will never forget one particularly gruelling Friday. (Afterwards I checked that it hadn't been Friday the 13th because of that day's misfortunes.) I was due to speak at a conference in Tasmania, and was scheduled to catch a plane from Sydney at 6:30am. This meant getting up at 4:30am. As I was muttering to God about how unfair it was, I got a phone call to say that I had been put on an *earlier* flight. It was then that I decided to take matters into my own hands.

I had a look at the conference program, and discovered that my speaking engagement was only at 2:00pm in the afternoon. Perfect! I would only need to catch a flight from Sydney at 10:00am. All of a sudden life was going my way!

So I duly arrived in Melbourne to catch my connecting plane to Tasmania, when things began to go wrong. My connection was one of those small planes, and despite no room in the overhead lockers for my bags, I made myself comfortable, and watched the propeller begin to turn. The problem, however, was the other propeller didn't.

Finally the captain politely broadcast that they had a "*minor* mechanical fault" and asked the passengers to be patient. I have flown enough times to know that 'minor' usually means *major* trouble.

The air-conditioning wasn't working so after some time – hot, sweaty and irritable – the passengers were asked to disembark and wait in the airport terminal. Almost an hour later, it dawned on me that I wasn't going to get to Tasmania on time for my speaking engagement. In fact, it didn't look like I was going to get to Tasmania *at all*. And even worse, it didn't look like I'd get home to Sydney either until Saturday morning.

I immediately contacted my colleagues in Tasmania, and they agreed it was a pointless exercise, so I went to book myself on the next flight back to Sydney. In spite of the frustrations of the day, I decided to look on the bright side: I would be home with my family on Friday night.

Yet the day wasn't over … not by a long shot. As I waited for my return flight, it was announced that this plane also had a "*minor* mechanical problem … ." I have never been one to let circumstances control me, so I made what I thought was an exceptionally smart move. Just in case … I went and booked myself on the *later* plane to Sydney as well. Whichever flight was going to leave first, I was going to be on it!

When all the passengers on the earlier flight were moved onto the later plane, I felt a sense of triumph. I was coming out on top. I was going to be in Sydney in less than 90 minutes … until I heard the captain's voice saying that "we have a minor problem with the automatic loading machine … ." Yet another *minor* problem!

Sitting on the plane while mechanics attempted to fix the problem, I watched dismally while the *later* flight to Sydney took off. In the end I did make it home that Friday night, but what a frustrating day of highs and lows!

No-one wakes up and thinks "I want to have a difficult day." They just happen. But you can lift the quality of your day and make it less difficult. If you are a person who despairs about your days, and loathes your life, you can change the nature of your day. How? I'm about to tell you.

Find a sponsor for your day

Your days are sponsored. You can live in the power and blessing of God, knowing that He is the one who called you to serve Him. He is consistent and faithful, no matter what happens during the course of your day.

You don't have to live on yesterday's blessings or worry about what is going to confront you tomorrow, because with God as your sponsor every day, He is the source of everything you need. He gives you your *daily* bread, His mercies are *new every morning* and His goodness and mercy shall follow you *all the days* of your life!

> From the rising of the sun to its going down the Lord's name is to be praised. [47]

You can praise your sponsor, the living God, when you are *in season* and *out of season*, through the good times and the tough times.

Talk to your day

Another key to great days is the way you speak to them. Don't underestimate the great power of the words you speak. I have mentioned people who say "This is just not my day" and I also find myself guilty of speaking things into my day that don't help at all.

There are people who put the power of a positive confession down to mind over matter or just hype, but there is great power in the way you speak. If you want to change your day, begin with changing the way you talk to, or about it. The theme of your heart will determine the words you speak:

> My heart is overflowing with a good theme; I recite my composition concerning the King. My tongue is the pen of a ready writer. [48]

A composition is a story, and the way you speak is the pen that writes the script to your story. Job said he loathed his life. If you keep saying "What a horrible day!" you can be sure it will turn out like that.

As you begin to change the way you speak to your day you will find you begin to feel better about it. Despite what is happening, remind yourself that this is *your* day! It is a gift from God.

Get to it

Most people go to work, but not everyone who works accomplishes much. There is a vast difference between a spirit that just clocks on and off, and a spirit that sees their day as a God-given opportunity to accomplish His purposes.

> Hard work has a future. Laziness pays off now.
> (Bumper sticker)

The way Jesus responded to His disciples' question about why a young boy was blind is significant:

> I must work the works of Him who sent Me while it is day; the night is coming when no one can work.[49]

Jesus was saying that this was an opportunity to bring light to a dark world, and while it was day, He needed to be doing what He was called to do on earth. If you want to change your day, you have to determine that every day is an opportunity to accomplish something for God.

Don't forget to stop

Do you know that in the six days of creation, God accomplished something every day? On the seventh day He accomplished something as well: He taught us all about rest. Some people don't know how to relax, although this is a spiritual principle:

> Six days you shall work, but on the seventh day you shall rest.[50]

Take control

There are many principles you can engage daily that will deliver the salvation that Christ has given you. If you use what Christ has given you, you can change your day.

> Behold, **now** is the accepted time; behold, **now** is the day of salvation. [51]

Now means *today*! If you want to change your day, make a decision to salvage it. The words '*salv*ation' and '*salv*age' both mean 'to rescue.'

> You cannot escape the responsibility of tomorrow by avoiding it today. — Abraham Lincoln

For example, if your financial situation is of great concern, decide that from *today* you are going to salvage it. Begin to avail yourself of Bible economics and simply do what the Word says.

If you want to improve your health (and therefore the condition of your life), apply Biblical principles so that you are free from worry, anxiety and living life on the edge of your nerves.

Laugh

Learn to laugh as this also will change your day. A merry heart does good like medicine. Quit worrying. It only makes one day seem like a thousand years.

Begin to change the quality of your future by approaching each day with a positive outlook.

CHANGE THE QUALITY OF EACH DAY

CHAPTER NINETEEN

CHANGE THE VALUE OF YOUR DAYS

Today I can get a thousand times more things done than I could some years ago. Recently I was in my office late one night and decided I needed some documents photocopied. I was about to go and do it when I realised that I didn't know how the photocopier worked! Even worse, I then realised that I didn't even know where the photocopier *was*!

Fortunately I have some wonderful staff who are able to get my photocopying done quickly and easily. This doesn't mean that I think that photocopying is beneath me. In 1983, when we started our church, I did everything. If I wanted some photocopying done, I did it myself. The reality is that today my time has become more valuable, and instead of spending hours in front of a photocopier machine, I have to be a better steward of my time.

Today I teach more people in one day than I did back when we started our church with 45 people. Besides ministering to our congregation of more than 10,000 people across our two congregations each weekend, there are also the thousands who watch our television program every week. God has truly increased and lifted the *value of my influence*, and I am very aware of being a good steward of each day.

One day as a thousand

One of my favourite scriptures is in Psalm 84. Look at how it describes the value of one day:

> For a day in Your courts is **better than a thousand**. I would rather be a doorkeeper in the house of my God than dwell in the tents of wickedness. [52]

The value of one day serving God is better than a thousand living any other lifestyle. It is not just as good as, but *better* than a thousand! (That is comparable to almost three years!)

This is a powerful principle in seeing increased influence and value across the parameters of your life – i.e. in terms of finance, time, influence and opportunity.

There are people in the world who earn in one day what most of us would earn in a thousand days. Imagine if you could earn one thousand times more than you do in one day (or if you earned in one day what would currently take you three years). I believe we need to see finance released into the Kingdom of God so we can fulfil His purposes. Most people think that to get more money, they would have to take an extra job, and work nights and weekends, but there is a better way. It's all about *learning to lift your value*.

You need to understand this principle in order to be more effective so you can live one day as a thousand. People often ask me how I fit all my local, national and international into my schedule.

You can build your life in such a way that what once took you a thousand days, you can now accomplish in one day. It amounts to building other people and resources around you, so that you don't try to do it all yourself.

Many people never learn the value of time, they never learn to utilise it effectively, and they end up wasting time doing things the way they always have done it. For this reason, they never progress beyond where they are.

Increasing the value of your day also includes making the most of special opportunities that present themselves. Day number 16,337 in my life was highly significant for me because I was invited to address the Prime Minister and Australian parliamentarians at the church service marking the opening of Parliament.

When it came to influencing secular Australia, in *one single day* I was able to accomplish more than I had in several thousand other days. I was able to bring the Word of the Lord to so many influential people in our nation.

It was a great day in my life, but why did they ask *me* to speak? Was it a lucky dip or did they pull my name out of the Yellow Pages? I think not. In terms of the span of my life, that particular day when I had the opportunity to speak to the parliamentarians, ambassadors and high court judges of our nation, was built on all the other 16,336 days that had gone before. It is the value of all those accumulated everydays that establishes your influence.

I believe God is wanting to do a quick work on the earth today. What used to take years to accomplish can now be done in moments. God is also wanting to use you. Don't waste your opportunity or let life pass you by.

Take control of your future, increase the value of each day and you will begin to live a life full of impact.

CHANGE
THE VALUE OF YOUR DAYS

PART FIVE

THE POWER TO CHANGE THE FUTURE

**The past cannot be changed.
The future is yet in your power.**

(Mary Pickford)

CHAPTER TWENTY

CHANGE THE IMPACT OF YESTERDAY ON TODAY

You have probably heard someone say, "don't put off until tomorrow what you can do today." It is amazing what people carry from one day into the next. What happened in the past doesn't belong in today and shouldn't be carried into your future. This is what the Bible says:

> Do not let the **sun go down** on your wrath. [53]

This scripture is talking about the end of a day. It's a simple verse, but it contains a powerful truth: don't carry over into tomorrow what is a negative leftover from today. To maximise the value of each day, don't waste your days on what is not relevant or important.

Many people are living ineffective lives because they have never learned to let the sun go down on certain things. For instance, someone in their forties may have experienced a tragic event, such as a divorce, in their twenties. Although they would have felt the hurt and pain back then, it happened almost half their life-time ago and should not have a hold on their life today.

The sad truth is that people still allow these events to rule their lives and affect their future. This is what Jesus said:

> Therefore do not worry about tomorrow, for tomorrow
> will worry about its own things. Sufficient for the day is
> its own trouble.[54]

Don't carry around baggage from ten or twenty years ago. Learn to put it to bed and refuse to take it into the rest of your life. In my various leadership roles, I have to make many major decisions each day. If my thinking was cluttered and consumed with past issues, I'd be unable to focus on the important issues of today.

> Make the mistakes of yesterday your lessons for today.
> (Source unknown)

The scripture tells us not to let the sun go down on our anger, but people also allow the sun to go down on unforgiveness, resentment, hurt, guilt and regret. If you bring those unresolved issues into the next day, they will begin to rule and affect your life. Deal with the issues of today *today*!

I'm not saying that you will wake up tomorrow and not feel hurt, but if you have made up your mind that it will not affect your future, you are on the road to breaking its power over your life.

Recognise the work of Christ, and His ability to lift you up and take you out of painful situations in the past. Aim to live your life the way God intends you to, not cluttered with junk that has nothing to do with today. Don't live on the leftovers. Make a decision that when the sun goes down tonight, it will not come up on those same negative things.

Look forward

By the time some great sport stars reach their mid-thirties, they begin to talk more of past victories and what happened when they were at their peak. Ultimately you find a few years later they retire and end up as TV commentators or motivational speakers.

The great thing about the Kingdom of God is that He wants

you to be a high achiever forever, and with Him you will never reach your peak. There is always something more to look forward to and strive for. He wants to take you onwards and upwards, stretching you so you keep moving to a higher level.

If someone only talks about the good old days, remembering past miracles and memorable services they attended, there is inevitably a lack of progress in their life today.

While the tests of the past bear testimony to the greatness of God, you have to keep focussed on the future, walking in faith step by step. It is good to look back and see how the Lord has brought you forward. We began our church in a hired hall, then moved to a warehouse, and then the Hills Entertainment Centre before we bought our own land and built a building. While reflection is good to see how far we have come, I spend a lot more time thinking about what is ahead.

My father is over seventy and I rarely hear him talking about the 'good old days,' even though he has seen plenty of them. He is still dreaming and moving forward with God, and there is no such thing as 'retirement' in his vocabulary.

The Kingdom of God is all about advancing. You cannot stay where you are now or hold on to the things of the past. God has so much more for you, plus He has put a lot of thought into your future.

Don't let long-gone events and the past affect your future. Remember not to let the sun go down on your wrath (or your resentment and regret) or allow it to rule your life any longer. Decide *now*, today, that the sun is not going to go down on it ever again and you will enter your tomorrow from a place of victory.

CHANGE
THE INFLUENCE OF YESTERDAY ON TODAY

CHAPTER TWENTY-ONE

CHANGE TO LIVE DAYS WITH HOPE

I completed Bible College at the age of 19, and went on to plant our church in Sydney when I was 29. I was full of hope, vision and enthusiasm, and that hope has never faded because it has been built on the promise and power of God. It is the resurrection life of Jesus that brings life and fulfilment to our length of days.

In a hopeless world, there is a God who promises "a future and a hope." No situation is too impossible for Him. We can live a certain time without food, a lot less time without water, but I don't believe we are meant to live without hope.

This **hope** we have as an anchor of the soul, both sure and steadfast. [55]

It is this hope that is like an anchor when we face challenge. The sad reality of age (and distance) is that many things deteriorate. Even the grass withers and flowers fade, but one thing is steadfast and sure: the Word of God abides forever, and our hope in Him is secure. If you build your days on the hope of God, no matter what situation confronts you, you will be anchored on the inside and able to overcome every challenge that tries to work against you.

Know your purpose

The key to harnessing your potential is to discover your particular gift and talent. These will present themselves as a strength in your life and God will most likely use you in that area.

> The purpose of life is a life of purpose. – Robert Byrne

I know what I am not good at. Besides photocopiers, I am too impatient with computers and I can't draw, but I know what I *can* do. I can communicate, motivate, and spot potential. These are gifts that God has put in my life and through the power of Jesus Christ, that is what I am anointed to do.

Don't try to be a square peg in a round hole. For example, if you are a financial whizz, are excellent with figures and making money, you are probably not called to be a preacher. Yet God's purpose for your life could be tremendous in raising money for Kingdom projects or helping with administration.

I believe that everyone of us has the potential to be great in the Kingdom of God and fulfil His purpose for our lives. You will hear about parents who put pressure on their children to be something other than what they want to be.

Don't get distracted or feel pressure from others to be what you are not called to be. Then, once you know what you are anointed to do, get down and do it.

Refuse to be intimidated by the limitations of others

Godly confidence is essential in stepping out and living life every day. Remember that it is not what *you* can do, but it is what *God* can do through you. Sadly, it is others who, out of their own insecurity, may try to bring you down to their size. If you listen and receive it, it may limit and hold you back.

In 1 Samuel chapter 10, we read how Saul changed dramatically as he was anointed with oil by the prophet Samuel:

> When they came there to the hill, there was a group of prophets to meet him; then the Spirit of God came upon him, and he prophesied among them. And it happened,

> when all who knew him formerly saw that he indeed
> prophesied among the prophets, that the people said to
> one another, "What is this that has come upon the son
> of Kish? Is Saul also among the prophets?" Then a man
> from there answered and said, "But who is their
> father?" Therefore it became a proverb: "Is Saul also
> among the prophets?"And when he had finished
> prophesying, he went to the high place. [56]

Until that time Saul had never prophesied before, so it was a bold move on his part when he went up to a group of well-known prophets and began to prophesy as well. Look at the attitude of those who knew him. They jeered at and questioned him.

You cannot live your life through the eyes of others. Fortunately Saul did the right thing – he went up to the high place. We need to know the power of spending time with Jesus in the high and secret place. No matter how busy you are, set aside time to get into the Word and to hear His voice, before you are faced with all the voices of doubt and confusion around you.

God wants to do a marvellous work in your life and you have to be positioned and ready to be raised up by Him. Building your relationship with God must be the priority of your day, because it will enable you to overcome any limitations.

See yourself as God sees you

The greatest key is to see yourself as God sees you – not as others do, or as you see yourself. As you allow God to change you, you will become unrecognisable to those who knew you before.

Look at what happened to Saul:

> So it was, when he had turned his back to go from
> Samuel, that God gave him another heart; and all
> those signs came to pass that day. [57]

Saul turned into another man that day and God gave him a new heart. From the very day that he was anointed by God, his life changed. He had woken up that day as usual and gone searching for donkeys. He was literally picked out of obscurity and launched into the purposes of God.

God can make you unrecognisable if you let Him change you. It doesn't mean you change your personality, but a new boldness and confidence will emerge as you step out of your comfort zone to serve the Lord. (Sadly, later in his life, Saul allowed this great start to be undone.)

If you remain faithful and in position, be ready because *your day* will come! Nevertheless, *today* is a special day because it is the one you are in. It is on today that you build the rest of your life.

CHANGE TO LIVE DAYS WITH HOPE

CHAPTER TWENTY-TWO

CHANGE THE IMPACT ON THE GENERATIONS

One day I went into an old stone church in a little village in southern England which had been built in the 12th century. Every vicar who had pastored that church over the past 900 years was listed on the wall. It was a substantially long list and I was interested to see that it revealed that some had been there a few months, most had been there several years, but amongst the names you would occasionally see someone who had pastored for 38 years or 41 years.

I was interested to see who had been there the longest and eventually found one who had pastored that village church for over sixty years. That pastor had spent his lifetime serving God in that village church.

In fact, each of those vicars had an impact, be it large or small, positive or negative, and their story will be told in eternity.

The great use of life is to spend it for something that will outlast it. – William James

You need to understand that your life is a lot bigger than you think it is. You are not just vapour, but you are on this earth for a purpose which goes well beyond you and your generation.

The day my father committed his life to Jesus, he didn't understand what was actually happening in terms of impacting other people's lives. Because of his decision, our family has been changed forever, and thousands of people have been trained up and are preaching the Gospel worldwide.

There have been some great men of God in days gone by – Wigglesworth, Finney, Spurgeon, Booth – but they are now in eternity. They made an impact during their generation but in all His wisdom, God chose to put you and me in this generation. You may imagine living in the time of horse-drawn carriages, but it isn't coincidence or chance you are here today. You are here for a time such as this to be part of God's eternal purpose.

> The only thing you take with you when you're gone is what you leave behind. – John Allston

The decisions you make and the actions you take have a huge impact, not only on yourself but on the generations to come. You will pass on a baton to the next generation. What will that baton look like?

In 1999, my father Frank decided to step back from the day-to-day running of his church, Sydney Christian Life Centre, and passed the baton of leadership on to me. What an honour for Bobbie and me to continue building on the foundations laid by my parents. It was also a tremendous responsibility as we were already pastoring Hills Christian Life Centre in Sydney's north west. Today Hillsong Church continues what was started in 1977, with our two major worship centres, a city-wide network of cells, and contributing services and ministries all adding to the expansion of future generations.

God thinks generationally

It is interesting that Matthew began writing his Gospel referring to the genealogy of Christ:

> The book of the generation of Jesus Christ, the son of

David, the son of Abraham. Abraham begot Isaac, Isaac begot Jacob, Jacob begot Judah and his brothers ...[58]

The Old Testament is full of genealogies, which you may have thought were unnecessary or dull, but the fact is that God always thinks and works generationally.

He was the God of Abraham, Isaac and Jacob, and instead of referring to Israel as a nation, they were always called the '*children* of Israel.' The Word continually speaks of life extending from one generation *to* another generation, rather than generation after generation:

One generation shall praise your works to another, and shall declare your mighty acts.[59]

We tend to think and focus on our lives in the here and now, but God was there from the beginning and He will be there at the end. He is omnipotent (all-powerful), omniscient (all-knowing) and omnipresent (everywhere). He is the God of the past, the present and the future.

We usually see life in terms of our own one dimension, but the Lord sees multi-dimensionally how the consequences affect generations ahead. He is not only looking at what is happening 'now' – He is looking way ahead.

Don't become so short-sighted that you cannot see beyond your own circumstances. You need to rise up and think well beyond your own life and begin to see that you are part of God's eternal plans that go from generation to generation. What God is wanting to build in your life doesn't just affect you, it affects the generation to come, even if you don't have any natural children in your life.

For instance, since 1989 people in our church have faithfully and consistently sown in financially to make possible a wonderful new church building. There are people who will enjoy the fruits of this building who aren't even born-again Christians yet. If we were small-minded and self-centred, we wouldn't be interested in expansion, yet these people were investing in the generations to come.

In writing Ecclesiastes, Solomon saw that without God, so many things in life are vain and futile. He was questioning the purpose of it all. This verse gives the answer: there is another generation coming!

> What profit has a man from all his labor in which he toils under the sun? One generation passes away, and another generation comes; but the earth abides forever.[60]

Although you may feel like Solomon did at times, frustrated and wondering what it is all about, the fact is that God saved you for a purpose. The Bible says that a good man leaves an inheritance to his children's children (Proverbs 13:22). I believe this goes a lot further than wealth or riches.

You can leave a great inheritance when you are aware that you are building a legacy for the generations ahead and have the opportunity to affect eternity.

CHANGE
THE IMPACT ON THE GENERATIONS

CHAPTER TWENTY-THREE

CHANGE THAT INFLUENCES OTHERS

The 'Great Australian Dream' is to own one's own home. People spend most of their adult lives striving so that when they reach middle-age, they have all their pensions and insurances in place, and have finally paid off their piece of land. They reach their life's goal, but what is next?

It is important to be practical about your future, but planning for yourself can be very 'self' focussed. God has a greater purpose for your life than that.

It is a wonderful adventure serving the Lord and we are living in a time of incredible opportunity. Our salvation in Christ goes beyond our own lives, because we are called to impact and influence others. For that reason we need to be positioned and ready to make a difference for the generations ahead.

Begin to also think generationally

It takes commitment to invest into new generations, and new generations are often hard to understand. Older generations may say, "It wasn't like that in our day!" Rather than being negative about the generation ahead or threatened by God raising up younger people, you need to be committed to the opportunity you have before you. Don't write off a younger generation just because they do things differently.

Even as a boy, Jesus did some outrageous things that *His* parents didn't understand. At the age of 12, He stayed behind in Jerusalem speaking to the teachers in the temple while His parents began the journey home. They went a whole day before they realised that they had lost God, and then took three days to find Him!

Today, young people are experiential and eccentric. They love extreme sports like bungee jumping, sky-diving or abseiling (I'm certain bungee jumpers leave their brains at the top!). I once stood and watched my son Ben bungee-jump from a very great height. He appeared totally fearless, and then couldn't understand why I declined his invitation to join him!

The funny thing about human nature is that it has to experience things. See a sign saying 'wet paint', and how compelled are we all to touch it?

Today young people like anything that pushes the limits. Now this can freak out an older generation, but turn those characteristics towards the purposes of God and it is a positive attribute. The best way to live a life of purpose is to have the kind of heart that is committed to building a platform and a way for those coming after us.

Live tall

People always presume that the generations are deteriorating or getting worse, but with the right input, they are becoming stronger. I look at young people today and see that they have confidence in areas I didn't have when I was 18. In many ways, young people today have gone forwards. There are things that my children talk about openly that in my time you just didn't mention.

When I was growing up, my parent's generation found it hard to publicly express true emotion and even holding hands in front of their children was a big deal. My generation was far more comfortable expressing emotions, but the younger generation is even less inhibited.

When the principles of God are at work, I believe a generation gets stronger. The Bible says that the seed of the upright will be blessed (Psalm 112:2).

Put the right ingredients and heritage into young people today and you build something powerful. As you get older, those you entrust with leadership may also be getting older, so it is important to make sure that you keep trusting younger people. At the age of 43, I was elected head of our group of churches in Australia and there were those who were horrified that one so young could lead over 900 churches. Yet the week before, a 43 year old was elected Prime Minister of Great Britain.

In recent times I have been actively releasing younger people into ministry within the life of our church, and I am inspired by their enthusiasm and zeal. That we can empower younger generations is an enormous privilege.

The Word says that we are a chosen generation and it is God's divine plan to build the generations. In the old days, the pioneers of the faith were persecuted and harassed. Because of their legacy, we are stronger.

Wisdom

Investing in the upcoming generations also requires godly wisdom. You cannot live thinking that life begins and ends with you.

This means lifting your thinking to the higher plain of God's thinking. He is very specific in how He sees the generations.

Moses led the Israelites out of Egypt with the purpose of leading God's people into the Promised Land. Forty years later he died in the wilderness and didn't personally see his dream come to pass, but God fulfilled the promise through the next generation – it was Joshua who led the children of Israel into Canaan.

In the same way, David dreamed of building a temple to worship God, but it was his son, Solomon, who built the magnificent temple in Jerusalem. It is interesting that the generation to come fulfilled the word that God had spoken to the generation before.

Serve your own generation

In serving the future, do not neglect to serve the present. In the midst of enthusiastic focus on the future, don't neglect your children or family. A godly inheritance is way more than a pile of money left after a relative's death.

> For David, after he had served his own generation by the will of God, fell asleep, was buried with his fathers, and saw corruption. [61]

The story of David didn't end when he died. He certainly made a lasting impact on the generations ahead, yet the scripture says that he served his own generation according to God's will. He probably didn't have us in mind when he killed Goliath or wrote the Psalms, yet his actions back then continue to affect the 21st century.

Called for a purpose

Many Christians are content to merely live with the knowledge of their eternal salvation, but it is important to get a revelation that we are not only *saved* but we are also *called* for a purpose:

> Therefore do not be ashamed of the testimony of our Lord, nor of me His prisoner, but share with me in the sufferings for the gospel according to the power of God, who has **saved us** and **called us** with a holy calling, not according to our works, but **according to His own purpose** and grace which was given to us in Christ Jesus before time began. [62]

God has called you to impact and influence the lives of others. Christianity is about much more than preparing for eternity, or retirement. This is *your* day. You are called to serve your own generation and in doing so, you will dramatically impact the future.

CHANGE THAT INFLUENCES OTHERS

CHAPTER TWENTY-FOUR

CHANGE YOUR COMMITMENTS

The vision to build our new church building is being fulfilled by the committed participation of our church members. Our God-given strategy involved raising up a 'company of 100 Kingdom People' who would lead by example in raising the finance required, together with an 'Army of Faithful Believers.' It has amazed and blessed me to see how our church has looked beyond themselves to sow into this vision.

A Kingdom spirit and a commitment to the future has enabled us to not only build our new facilities with current trends in mind, but what we are building is a church for the future generations. It is when you begin to *see beyond yourself* that you can commit to changing the future for others.

A commitment to see

Every time we take up an offering for our church building program, some people see it as an incredible opportunity to reach more people who are in need of a Saviour. But sadly there are those who only see somebody asking for money again. What is in their heart interprets how they see things.

Earlier chapters looked at how the theme of your heart

determines the course you take and how you see the future. Commitment is a heart issue, and Jesus said, "Blessed are the pure in heart for they shall *see* God."

You can come under the sound of the Word of God but unless your heart is open to receive, you will perceive it from where you stand.

> Therefore I speak to them in parables, because seeing they do not see, and hearing they do not hear, nor do they understand. And in them the prophecy of Isaiah is fulfilled, which says: 'Hearing you will hear and shall not understand, and seeing you will see and not perceive.'[63]

David could not have served his generation so magnificently if he couldn't see God or His purpose. If your heart is cluttered with things that prevent you from seeing and hearing God, you won't fulfil what God has called you to do. It is by looking beyond yourself and having a bigger vision than your own life, that you will gain a pure heart that will clearly *see* the will of God.

Commitment to innovation

Back in the 1990s, when Hillsong Music Australia began to record praise and worship music, we faced tremendous obstacles. I remember one of the top men in the Australian 'Christian' music industry telling me that "live praise and worship doesn't sell." There were others who suggested that we package it as youth music, but we pressed on and ran with our vision. Since then we have proved that live praise and worship music is a blessing to the whole body of Christ.

Most people live within their set paradigm structure and resist anything new. If you live with a commitment to innovation and new ideas, you will be challenged and opposed by those who only see the world their way.

For instance, the man who invented watches without moving parts took his invention to the established Swiss watchmakers. They rejected his invention because according to them, a watch without moving parts wasn't a watch. They couldn't accept it. However Seiko, the Japanese company, picked up the idea and ran with it. They revolutionised the watch industry and almost put the Swiss watch companies out of business. All it took was a paradigm shift and ability to see beyond what was in existence.

If you are going to be innovative, you cannot expect everybody to understand and embrace your vision, because most times, the establishment won't. When Jesus lived on earth as a man, He didn't fit the paradigm of the religious people then, which is why the scribes and Pharisees continually persecuted Him. They were offended by His teachings and opposed Him because His teachings didn't fit into the rules by which they saw the world.

If you are committed to changing the future, you cannot be reliant on old ideas or established methods. Have the courage to be innovative and step out, despite what those around you may say. Although there will be obstacles along the way, don't lose your vision and commitment to being innovative for the Kingdom of God. You have to be prepared to press through.

Commitment to the right vehicle

When I was a little boy, I had a scooter. As I got a little older, I rode a three-wheeled trike before I got my first bicycle. One day my father took me down to the shops and as I sat impatiently waiting for him in the car, all of sudden he came around the corner with a shining green bicycle. It was my pride and joy. Of course getting my first car was an unforgettable moment in my life. It was a '57 Austin A50. It was also green and it cost me $650.

Many people desire to make an impact on the generations but rely on old vehicles to get there. Imagine me trying to fulfil my overseas speaking engagements via my original scooter or bicycle! You need the right vehicle and the right associations to enable God to take you forward. You may have a great vision to impact the earth, but alone you cannot do as much as you could together with others. If you are in associations which are holding you back or on a vehicle that is moving too slowly, stretch yourself by stepping into the mainstream and being committed to going forward.

I have been blessed to pastor at least four world-class songwriters, and many others heading in the same direction. I cannot take credit for their anointing or their God-given gifts, but I do have a sense of satisfaction about their opportunity. The Hillsong Church is a vehicle that has taken their songs to the world. One of these writers, who severed their link to our church several years ago, told me how they were writing more songs than ever before. Interestingly, it is only the songs that were written within the local church that I have heard anybody singing. It seems as though the local church was the vehicle which God was blessing.

Currently, the most sung praise and worship songs in Australian churches have emerged from the life of our church. Obviously that association with Hillsong Church has been very fruitful for people like Darlene Zschech, Reuben Morgan and Russell Fragar. They have obvious talent, a beautiful anointing, but also the *right vehicle*. Talent and anointing on their own aren't enough, but placing the *right people*, in the *right place*, at the *right time*, has enormous potential.

A commitment to the harvest

When we built phase one of our church building, there were those who wondered why we needed to build a bigger one for phase two. They couldn't see the harvest ahead. Three years later we were overcrowding that building several times each weekend. Being committed to serving your own generation and the generations ahead, you have to think bigger, step out and be ready for the harvest. The disciples of Jesus learnt the hard way.

> When He had stopped speaking, He said to Simon, "Launch out into the deep and let down your nets for a catch." But Simon answered and said to Him, "Master, we have toiled all night and caught nothing; nevertheless at Your word I will let down the net." And

when they had done this, they caught a great number of fish, and their net was breaking. So they signaled to their partners in the other boat to come and help them. And they came and filled both the boats, so that they began to sink. [64]

Notice that Jesus told Simon to let down their nets (plural), but Simon agreed to let down a net (singular). In spite of hearing the Lord's instruction, they decided to play it safe, and cautiously only let down one net. It almost sank the boats.

Think about all the work the fishermen had after they hauled in that massive harvest of fish. They would have required cleaning, gutting, and cooking. There are those who would sink if God released to them all that He has prepared for them, because they are not ready for all the work involved.

In terms of our building project, people who questioned phase two were really asking "What is wrong with one net?" But the Lord has planned a harvest and when He releases it, we will be ready for it.

There is no room for small thinking or pettiness. When opportunity faces you, you have to be ready. If you want to see generations impacted for the Kingdom of God, you have to become a bigger thinker, step out and have the nets ready. You have to open your life up to expect the harvest.

CHANGE YOUR COMMITMENTS

CHAPTER TWENTY-FIVE

CHANGE YOUR PRIORITIES

God took a young Bible college student and is fulfilling the dreams he had as a young boy: to pastor a great church and to be a leader in the Body of Christ. All I did was make Him my priority, and seek first the Kingdom.

Now after more than 25 years in ministry, imagine if I walked on to the platform, and because of ill health, I was unable to speak. I fly all over the world and lead a full and busy life. I need to be fit and healthy to fulfil my purpose. One of my greatest commitments is making *healthy living* a priority.

Make health a priority

If you are going to fulfil your God-given purpose, it helps to be strong and healthy, both physically and emotionally. I believe prevention is better than cure, so you need to look after yourself.

Don't miss your chance. The Word describes how fish are caught in a net and birds caught in a snare (Ecclesiastes 9:12). Rather than swimming with ease the way God intended, a fish caught in a net will use all its energy and resources to break free. It is the same as a bird caught in a snare. That is exactly what the enemy wants to do – trap you in a snare that makes you ineffective.

This isn't about vanity or what you look like – it is about being committed to your call and purpose. The enemy will definitely try and steal your health, if you give him the opportunity. Don't give him a helping hand, but do what you need to keep yourself in good shape.

In the same way, people get emotionally involved in all sorts of situations, and instead of being able to help others, need help themselves. Break free of the nets and snares that are holding you down, so you can live an effective life.

If the enemy can keep you sick, or in an emotional mess with a depressed spirit, he will. The good news is that the Bible says that whom the Son sets free is free indeed. Begin to live in the freedom of the Holy Spirit and co-operate with God so you can have a mighty impact on your own generation and the generations ahead.

Take the words of Christ seriously

Jesus made some incredible statements. One thing He said was:

> Most assuredly, I say to you, he who believes in Me, the works that I do he will do also; and greater works than these he will do, because I go to My Father.[65]

What a profound statement! What Jesus said was that we would not only do the works that He did, but we would do *greater* works. That is a huge challenge. He healed the sick, fed thousands and raised the dead.

If we are going to take His Word seriously, we need to seriously engage the tools that He has given us to accomplish such things. In Acts chapter one, it says that you will receive power when the *Holy Spirit* comes upon you and you will be witnesses in Jerusalem, Judea, Samaria and to the ends of the earth.

In the time of Jesus, transportation enabled him to impact the area around Jerusalem, Judea and Samaria. Paul went even further, considering what was available to him, but by no means did he reach the ends of the earth. He spread the Gospel throughout the Middle Eastern region, to Malta, Crete, Italy and Greece.

But this is *our* time, and we can go further. Today we can get on an aeroplane and go to the ends of the earth if we have to – to northern Alaska or Invercargill at the southernmost point of New Zealand. Jesus spoke to a crowd of 5,000 but the meetings we have today can be broadcast live via satellite or the internet.

I remember when I was a teenager how fantastic it was to be able to watch a special 'live' broadcast on TV as the All Blacks rugby team played on the other side of the world. Now it is an everyday occurrence on television. We can watch sport, world news, even wars, as they happen.

The world may think that aeroplanes and technology are there for their use, but they are great resources for the Kingdom of God. Just as the enemy tries to use things for evil, we are able to use them for good.

When Jesus preached the sermon on the mount, He didn't have a cordless microphone or a sound system. The people never sat on comfortable chairs. If we begin to expand our thinking, and use the resources and tools available to us, we can do greater exploits for the Kingdom, just as Jesus said we would.

Make the fullness of the Gospel your priority

Around the world, God is doing incredible things, but you need to remember why. Jesus declared that the Spirit of the Lord was upon Him *because* ... and went on to say why:

> The Spirit of the Lord is upon Me, because He has anointed Me to preach the gospel to the poor; He has sent Me to heal the brokenhearted, to proclaim liberty to the captives and recovery of sight to the blind, to set at liberty those who are oppressed; To proclaim the acceptable year of the Lord.[66]

The church is not just a meeting place for Christians to congregate. Of course it is where we receive fellowship, support and teaching, but if we are going to impact generations and reach others, we cannot be introspective. God has called us to look well beyond ourselves.

There are so many opportunities to help the needy and the poor. Whether you are giving, praying, or going yourself, you need to remember that the Great Commission is not to bless us, but for us to bless and make a difference to the generations.

God's will for your life goes beyond you. There are many scriptures that teach us to reach the poor, and this just doesn't mean those who are financially poor. There are people who are wealthy in terms of money, but are poor on the inside, when it comes to relationships and inner peace.

Look out for opportunities that enable you to reach others. As long as you have breath, you are called to serve the Lord. During church services, there are faithful workers who are sowing into the lives of babies and little children, teaching them the Word. Those little children will have the Word imprinted on their mind forever because of that.

As the bigger picture of your life emerges, I encourage you to keep yourself stretched and challenged by putting your priorities in order and putting the Kingdom of God first in your life. That is what changing the future is all about.

CHANGE YOUR PRIORITIES

CONCLUSION

Never be afraid to trust an unknown future to a known God

(Corrie Ten Boom)

CONCLUSION

I like the following story about a man who *changed the world*: Once upon a time a man set out to change the world. Before long he discovered that the world was far too big for one person to change. So he decided to change his country. Crooked politicians and special interest groups unfortunately thwarted his efforts, so he decided to change his neighbourhood. But his neighbours simply closed their doors and shut their windows, so he decided to change his family. Instead of changing, his children rebelled and his wife threatened a divorce, and things only got worse.

Finally, the man decided to change himself. And when he did that, he changed the world.

Change starts with you and me.

Past, Present and Future

Jesus Christ is the same yesterday, today, and forever. [67]

Because of Jesus Christ, you have the power to change your future and you can look forward to everything that lies ahead. What He did on the cross, and what He does in you today is what builds your future.

YOU

It all depends on *you*. You have to turn the key to open the door to a new, exciting future.

It is within the power of your hand not only to change your own life, but also to impact the lives of others. As you change, you will begin to see situations, circumstances and other people begin to change too. No matter what position you may find yourself in today, you have choices before you that can affect the rest of your life.

CAN

The word *can* is full of potential. It means you have the opportunity and the capacity to take action and accomplish something positive. You are a success waiting to happen – you just have to believe you can do it, and half the battle is won.

CHANGE

Change is all about altering your course, transforming your attitudes and modifying your methods. It means that you cannot stay the same, because you switch from what was to something new.

THE FUTURE

The future is anytime after now! It is what is yet to come, what is still ahead of you. This is when expectation and anticipation comes into the equation, because once YOU realise that you CAN make things happen that can CHANGE a situation, your FUTURE and destiny in God is an exciting surprise waiting to happen!

My prayer is that this book will challenge and inspire you to press forward into God's awesome plan for your life. As you apply the principles and wisdom of the Word, it will begin to change your life dramatically. I encourage you to always remember that God's plans and purposes go well beyond you. Go and live a life of increasing influence and impact, and ultimately we will make a difference in our world.

YOU CAN CHANGE THE FUTURE!

FOOTNOTE REFERENCES

1. Jeremiah 29:11
2. Psalm 45:1
3. Proverbs 16:9
4. Psalm 16:7
5. Proverbs 4:23
6. Matthew 12:35
7. 1 Peter 5:8
8. 2 Corinthians 2:10,11
9. Ephesians 4:27
10. Luke 17:1
11. Proverbs 12:25
12. Psalm 16:5
13. Isaiah 55:11
14. Proverbs 11:14
15. Psalm 1:1
16. Isaiah 55:8,9
17. Proverbs 14:12
18. James 1:14
19. Mark 4:24
20. John 16:33
21. Philippians 3:14
22. Psalm 78:8,9
23. Proverbs 28:13
24. Luke 14:18
25. Luke 14:19
26. Luke 14:20
27. Psalm 139:1
28. 1 Samuel 16:7
29. Romans 14:12
30. Acts 3:19
31. Luke 18:10-13
32. Ecc 12:13,14
33. Romans 1:16
34. Romans 2:16
35. Luke 8:12
36. Jeremiah 17:11
37. Psalm 142:7
38. 2 Corinthians 5:17
39. Psalm 112:1-5
40. Proverbs 22:6
41. Ezekiel 18:2
42. Ezekiel 18:20
43. Psalm 90:12
44. Psalm 118:24
45. Proverbs 27:1
46. Ecclesiastes 1:5
47. Psalm 113:3
48. Psalm 45:1
49. John 9:4
50. Exodus 34:21
51. 2 Corinthians 6:2
52. Psalm 84:10
53. Ephesians 4:26
54. Matthew 6:34
55. Hebrews 6:19
56. 1 Samuel 10:10-13
57. 1 Samuel 10:9
58. Matthew 1:1,2
59. Psalm 145:4
60. Ecclesiastes 1:3-4
61. Acts 13:36
62. 2 Timothy 1:9
63. Matthew 13:13,14
64. Luke 5:4-7
65. John 14:12
66. Luke 4:18,19
67. Hebrews 13:8

For further information on other books and resource material
by Brian Houston, write to:
Maximised Leadership Inc.
PO Box 1195, Castle Hill NSW 1765 Australia